Hebrew Academy of West Queens

The Hebrew Academy of West Queens was established to perpetuate the traditional ideals of our heritage, to teach Torah to our children, so that they will have both the inspiration and understanding to live as observant Jews. From its inception, the Yeshiva has been in the forefront of the "kiruv" movement, igniting the flame of Yiddishkeit in thousands of American public school and immigrant children who would have been lost to assimilation.

Over the past twenty-eight years, the school has provided thousands of these children with a Torah true education. Its graduates have become outstanding students in many of the well-known Yeshiva institutions. The two-hundred and seventy students currently enrolled in the Yeshiva in Jackson Heights come from neighborhoods throughout the metropolitan area.

What distinguishes the Hebrew Academy of West Queens from Yeshivas that cater exclusively to immigrant children? At the Hebrew Academy immigrant children are placed in a setting where they interact with and learn from veteran Yeshiva students. Immigrant students who have already become Torah oriented have a very positive effect on new arrivals. The Yeshiva and its dedicated staff impart our heritage in an environment where both advanced and beginning students from all backgrounds and cultures can flourish.

34-25 82nd Street / Jackson Heights N.Y. 11372 / (718) 899-9192

A few short months ago, this boy had not yet seen the Alef-Beis.
Now he can daven from a siddur.

One of our alumni has returned to help a younger student — his cousin.

Soon, the newcomers are ready to enter into our mainstream classes.

הסטוריה

The ArtScroll History Series®

Rabbis Nosson Scherman / Meir Zlotowitz
General Editors

The Unconquerable Spirit

The Unconquerable Spirit

Vignettes of
The Jewish Religious Spirit
The Nazis Could Not Destroy

Compiled by
SIMON ZUKER

Translated and Edited by
GERTRUDE HIRSCHLER

Published by

ZACHOR INSTITUTE

Distributed by

Mesorah Publications, ltd.

Publishers of
The ArtScroll Series®

New York
1980

FIRST EDITION
First Impression . . . May, 1980
SECOND EDITION
Revised and Corrected
First Impression . . . May, 1981
Second Impression . . . July, 1990

Published and Distributed by
MESORAH PUBLICATIONS, Ltd.
Brooklyn, New York 11232

Distributed in Israel by
MESORAH MAFITZIM / J. GROSSMAN
Rechov Harav Uziel 117
Jerusalem, Israel

Distributed in Europe by
J. LEHMANN HEBREW BOOKSELLERS
20 Cambridge Terrace
Gateshead, Tyne and Wear
England NE8 1RP

Distributed in Australia & New Zealand by
GOLD'S BOOK & GIFT CO.
36 William Street
Balaclava 3183, Vic., Australia

Distributed in South Africa by
KOLLEL BOOKSHOP
22 Muller Street
Yeoville 2198
Johannesburg, South Africa

ARTSCROLL HISTORY SERIES *
THE UNCONQUERABLE SPIRIT

ISBN
0-89906-202-4 (hard cover)
0-89906-203-2 (paperback)

Typography by Compuscribe at ArtScroll Studios, Ltd.
4401 Second Avenue / Brooklyn, N.Y. 11232 / (718) 921-9000

Printed in the United States of America by Moriah Offset
Bound by Sefercraft, Quality Bookbinders, Ltd. Brooklyn, N.Y.

Table of Contents

ACKNOWLEDGMENT

We gratefully acknowledge the untiring efforts of Mr. Chaim Rotner and Rabbi Leibel Cywiak regarding the publication of this volume.

Introduction

The annals of the Nazi Holocaust are replete with accounts of Jewish heroism. Jews of every shade of political opinion and religious belief showed to the world how brave men and women fought against the forces of incredible evil and how they met their death as proud martyrs for a sacred heritage. The record has been set down in innumerable books, essays and articles.

Very little, however, has been written in English about the heroism of one particular group: the saintly, devout Orthodox Jews of Eastern Europe. This small book is a modest attempt to fill that gap. The authors whose work has been gathered in this volume give testimony to the life, and the death, of men, women and children who until the end never ceased to proclaim, in word and deed, their undying belief in God and in His righteousness.

Some of them believed in waging an active struggle against the Nazi enemy: the "Partisan Rebbe" and Rabbi Menahem Zemba, to cite only two examples, helped their fellow Jews organize armed resistance. Others believed that their best weapon against evil would be to lead lives of goodness and saintliness that would serve as an inspiration to future generations. Thus we see "Samson the Mighty" adhering to all the details of Sabbath observance even in a forced labor camp, and rabbis in the ghetto making sure that the minutiae of dietary laws and Passover regulations were followed in the face of unbelievable odds. Scholars and simple folk bonded together in ghettoes and concentration camps to study the Law of God; bunkers and underground shelters were turned into informal Talmudic academies.

Even in death these pious men, women and children were not divided: they agreed that if they had to give up their lives they would do so not in cringing despair, but with quiet pride and dignity, declaring the praise of God even as they boarded trains for Treblinka or dug their own graves beneath the muzzles of Nazi guns.

This book ends with "The Perfect Memorial," the story of how, even as he went to his death, a humble Jew found it in his heart to seek a way of perpetuating the memory of his own martyrdom that would serve as a blessing to generations yet unborn.

Over three decades have gone by since then. A whole new generation has grown up in a climate where Auschwitz is considered a thing of the past. But even for today's generation of Jews, Auschwitz represents a stunning personal loss: the Nazi Holocaust has deprived millions of Jewish men and women alive today of the parents, grandparents and mentors who might have inspired their offspring and their disciples to lead the lives of piety and saintliness for which they had become bywords in Jewish history.

If this book will help recapture the memory and the teachings of the martyrs who lived and died with the Word of God in their thoughts and upon their lips, the authors and editors who participated in this project will feel richly rewarded.

I consider it a great privilege to have helped prepare this volume for publication.

GERTRUDE HIRSCHLER

Foreword

Much has already been written about the Holocaust, dealing with suffering and pain, brutality and agony. The Zachor Institute is concerned with the recounting the incidents of Kiddush HaShem — sanctification of God — that took place in the ghettoes and the camps where, despite fear, pain, hunger, and other forms of suffering, Jews did not discredit their being made in the image of God. Religious Jews did not lose their faith in God, nor their reliance upon Him.

These incidents are seldom noted in the Holocaust literature. The Zachor Institute seeks to make you conscious of the tragic day-to-day lives of Jews in ghettoes and concentration camps, particularly how religious Jews lived and behaved throughout the war years until the moment of their annihilation.

In this fashion you will not forget, and will be able to transmit this to future generations. For example, I will share with you a sorrowful episode of ghetto life:

Late one night in 1943 I heard the sound of a child's bitter wailing coming from my neighbor's apartment. Curious, I knocked at the door. An eight-year-old girl with a chalk-white face was crying anguishedly, "Tateshi, give me something to eat! I'm so-o-o hungry." The poor child's parents were heartbroken but they had nothing to give her, for this was the last night before the weekly food ration.

I hugged the crying girl to my heart and tried to comfort her, "Your crying has surely been heard up in Heaven, and that's where help will come from."

The child opened her dark, charming eyes wide and asked, "So I won't have to cry again?" And she fell asleep in my arms.

I am aware that reading about the Holocaust will break your heart, but there is nothing more wholesome than a broken heart.

SIMON ZUCKER

The Unconquerable Spirit

1.

Leaders of Their People

The Partisan Rebbe

Heroes of the Spirit

The Nazi Purim Party

Rabbi Shmuel Shelomo Leiner

THE UNCONQUERABLE SPIRIT

The Partisan Rebbe

R. Shmuel Shelomo Leiner, the last rebbe
of Radzin (Lublin Province), was one of the
youngest Hasidic rebbes in Poland. His
grandfather, R. Gershon Henoch Leiner, had
caused a sensation in the Hasidic world dur-
ing the latter part of the 19th century with his
announcement that he had rediscovered
tekheleth, the blue dye used in Biblical times
for the threads of the tzizith, the ritual
fringes which the Torah bids every male Jew to
wear. The old rebbe had even set up a
laboratory to produce the dye for use by his
disciples. His grandson and spiritual heir was
no less gifted with daring and initiative, but
he employed these talents for a purpose
which even R. Gershon would have been
hard put to visualize.

W hen World War II broke out, R. Shmuel Shelomo
Leiner left his home town and settled in nearby
Vladova. In the summer of 1942, when the news of the
mass murder of Jews in the death camps first leaked out,
the young *rebbe* called a meeting of his friends and disciples. From that meeting, the word went forth to the villages, ghettoes and labor camps that the *rebbe* did not
wish his Jews to go to their death like so many sheep to
the slaughterhouse. Instead, he urged them to take to the
woods and join the partisans in their fight against the
Germans.

The *rebbe* himself laid plans for an organized armed revolt by his Hasidim in the labor camps. The uprising in one camp was preceded by a day of fasting and prayer. At the midnight hour following the fast, the Hasidim set fire to the barracks, then took up arms and began to shoot at the German guards. In the chaos that ensued, hundreds of inmates managed to escape into the woods surrounding the camp.

Alas, the victory of the insurgents was short-lived. The Germans quickly recovered from their initial surprise and opened fire on the fugitives. Dozens of Jews were killed; others gave up the struggle and returned to the camp, where the Nazis punished them cruelly.

But this setback did not stop the *rebbe* from making new plans for revolts and mass escapes.

In due time it came to the ears of the Gestapo that the driving force behind the outbreaks in the labor camps was a rabbi who could command the blind obedience of his disciples. The Gestapo men scoured the surrounding villages and ghettoes for the "rebel rabbi." When the Germans finally narrowed down their search to the town of Vladova, they let it be known that if the rabbi would not be delivered to them by nightfall, all the Jews of Vladova would be put to death.

The *rebbe*, ensconced in a hideaway prepared by his Hasidim, was unaware that the entire community was in danger because of him. But R. Shmuel's *gabbai* (assistant), R. Yehoshua-Wolf, realized that quick action was needed if his master and his community were to be saved from death. Draped in his long *tallith*, R. Yehoshua-Wolf reported to Gestapo headquarters and announced that he, Yehoshua-Wolf, was the *rebbe* of Radzin for whom the Germans had been looking. The Germans took his word without question and shot him right then and there.

Before long, however, the Gestapo discovered that

they had shot the wrong man. Once again they had
Vladova surrounded by a contingent of Germans; this
time, they gave the Jews only two hours to produce their
rabbi, if they wanted to remain alive. Somehow, R.
Shmuel learned what had happened, and he understood
that unless he gave himself up, his Hasidim were lost.
Ashen-faced, he arose from his bench, put on his shrouds,
his father's white cap and his *tallith*, with his grandfather's blue fringes. Thus attired, he left his hiding place
and walked through the streets of the town to the headquarters of the Gestapo.

After days of incredible torture, he was taken into the
courtyard of Gestapo headquarters and shot. The date of
his death was the Sabbath, eve of the New Moon of the
month of Sivan, 5702, or May 16, 1942.

> — *Based on article by S.Z. Shragai in* HaTzofeh,
> *Sivan 1, 5706 (1946).*

Rabbi Baruch Safrin

Heroes of the Spirit

The rabbis and rebbes of countless communities in Eastern Europe proved themselves true heroes during the Holocaust period. By their active concern for each and every one of their followers, and by the example they set by their own conduct, they won the respect even of many who were far removed from their own way of thinking.

Abish Suess of Tel Aviv related how R. Baruch Safrin, the last of the *rebbes* of Komarno, sold or bartered his own household goods to procure food for the starving Jews of his ghetto community.[1]

In the town of Wleczka near Vilna there was a labor camp where Jews performed slave labor under the command of the German district commissioner. Near the camp was a bombed-out house, where the town's rabbi, R. Moshe Klein, gathered his disciples every day to recite psalms and pray for the speedy deliverance of the Jewish people. Over and over he was asked to tell when Israel's sufferings would come to an end, and he always replied by citing the text from the Book of Psalms: "Until when will Thy strength be in captivity and Thy glory in the hands of the enemy? They will be put to shame and will fall from their strength." And then he added: "Deliverance is sure to come; even if it tarries, let us not despair but wait patiently for it."[2]

The *rebbes* sought to impress upon their followers

that death with pride was preferable to a life without purpose or content. Arriving in Treblinka, the last of the *rebbes* of Piotrkov-Trybunalski said to the others who had shared his boxcar: "It is better to die alive than to live dead."[3]

When the Germans came to the *rebbe* of Lukow to take him away, the *rebbe* donned his shrouds, bade farewell to his family and followed the Germans as far as the door of his house. Then he stopped and refused to move any further. Later, his bullet-riddled corpse was found in front of his house.

A young Hasidic leader in Lukow (his father was Peretz Lieberman, a member of Lukow's *Judenrat**) learned that, in return for a bribe, the Germans might consider stopping the deportation of Jews from the town. The younger Lieberman managed to raise the required amount. But by the time the Germans, accompanied by Ukrainian policemen, arrived at his house to collect the money, he had learned that the Germans had no intention of keeping their part of the bargain. "So you want to kill us and get paid for it, too?" Lieberman shouted at the Germans. With that, he pulled the banknotes from his pocket, tore them into shreds and flung himself upon the nearest German. He would have choked the Nazi, had not one of the Ukrainians pulled his gun and shot Lieberman killing him instantly.[4]

"On October 2, 1942," a survivor of the Frampol ghetto recalls, "the Nazis surrounded our ghetto. We had already known for several days that our deportation was imminent and so we called a conference of our leaders — Rabbi Judah Lerner, Reb Yaakov Baruch (a *shohet*), Gershon Rosenberg, my own father, and a few other notables — to decide what we should do. What would be the braver course to follow: come before the Germans and report for deportation, or wait for the Germans to come

* Governing body of the ghetto.

and get us? The *shohet* held that we should report for deportation of our own free will, to show by our own example how Jews — men, women and children — were ready to face martyrdom. But the majority disagreed; in their view the same purpose could be accomplished by going about our usual activities and waiting for the Germans to take us."[5]

Early in January, 1943, the local Gestapo chiefs appeared at the offices of the *Judenrat* in Ostrowiec and demanded that the rabbi of Ostrowiec, R. Yechezkel — they referred to him as the "miracle-working rabbi" — should be turned over to them by noon. If this were not done, the entire Jewish community would suffer.

The Rabbi of Ostrowiec

This command from the Gestapo set off panic among the Jews. They pondered ways of saving their rabbi by hiding him, bribing the Nazis or helping him escape from the ghetto. But the rabbi did not concern himself with such things: he went to the *mikvah* to purify himself, put on his white shrouds, then donned his *tallith* and phylacteries, and prayed for hours on end.

Literally minutes before the deadline, some Jews, at the risk of their own lives, offered to help the rabbi escape to the "Aryan" side of the city. But the rabbi would not hear of it. "Far be it from me," he said, "to endanger the lives of the 30,000 Jews who are still living in this city. If I were to run away, the Nazis would take their revenge on these innocent people. It is better that I should be sacrificed for my community than my community should perish on my account."

And so the rabbi marched up to the headquarters of the *Judenrat* and announced that he was ready go with the Germans. Twenty Jews pleaded with the Germans to kill them but to let their rabbi live. "Very well, then," the Gestapo chief said, "you'll die — along with your rabbi." He ordered his men to seize the 20 Jews and then commanded the rabbi to stand against the wall of the synagogue square. After shooting the rabbi, the Nazis ordered the other 20 to dig a grave for him, and for themselves as well. Then the 20 men were gunned down and thrown into the mass grave.

"My own father," the survivor who told us this story recalled, "had contacted the bishop of Tzozmir (Sandomierz) and begged him to hide the rabbi of Ostrowiec. The bishop had actually agreed to remove the rabbi from the ghetto and to give him shelter for the duration of the war, but when my father informed the rabbi of the bishop's offer, he said that he would not save his own skin while his community perished."[6]

Rabbi Israel Shapiro — Rabbi of Grodzisk

For 48 years R. Israel Shapiro, the *rebbe* of Grodzisk Mazowiecki, had been the respected leader of a community of Hasidim in Warsaw. After the outbreak of the war, his disciples abroad explored every possible way of rescuing their spiritual mentor. They even sent him a passport and immigration documents from a neutral country, but R. Israel refused to leave his Hasidim in the Warsaw ghetto.

And so R. Israel was among the thousands who were herded into boxcars and transported from Warsaw to the death camp of Treblinka. When the deportation train arrived at Treblinka, the Hasidim who had made the journey with him asked their *rebbe* what he thought of the situation now.

"Listen to me, brothers and sisters," the *rebbe* calmly replied. "We are children of the people of God. We must not rebel against the ways of the Lord. These, our sufferings, are meant to precede the coming of the Messiah. If it was decreed that we should be the victims of the Messianic throes, that we should go up in flames to herald the redemption, then we should consider ourselves fortunate to have this privilege. Our ashes will serve to cleanse the people of Israel who will remain and so our death will hasten the day when the Messiah will appear. Therefore, brothers and sisters, let not your spirits falter. As you walk into the gas chambers, do not weep but rejoice."

With their heads held high, the *rebbe* of Grodzisk Mazowiecki and his disciples from the Warsaw ghetto entered the gas chambers, singing the hymn *Ani Ma'amin* [7]:

> I believe, I believe,
> With perfect faith,
> In the coming of the Messiah.
> And even if he should tarry,
> I will await his coming every day ...

(Shmuel Niger, Kiddush Hashem, p. 361.)

The Nazi "Purim Party"

The agony of R. Judah Leib Eisenberg, the rabbi of the little Polish town of Lask, began soon after the Germans came. It mirrored a fiendishness rarely equalled even in the records of Nazi barbarism, and at the same time an almost superhuman greatness seldom encountered even in centuries of Jewish martyrdom.

One day toward the end of winter the German commander of the area paid a visit to the rabbi of Lask. "Rabbi," he said, "I understand that you will have a very joyful holiday soon. It's called Purim, isn't it? Well, we Germans would like to celebrate Purim together with the Jews this year. You Jews hanged the prime minister of the king of Persia, didn't you? So it is only fair that we should have our own little hanging party for you. But we Germans will be more charitable than your ancestors were. You executed not only Haman but also his ten sons. All we want is to hang two Jews — just two, mind you. My request to you, my dear rabbi, is a very simple one. I want you to select the two Jews we are going to hang. We will be glad to accept whoever you will turn over to us. I will give you three days to make your selection."

For a few moments the rabbi was stunned. But when he regained his senses, his voice was steady and clear.

"I do not need three days, *Herr Kommandant,*" he said. "I have already made my selection. You said you wanted two Jews. Very well; I myself will be the first, and my wife will be the second. I will not give you any other Jews to kill."

Rabbi Judah Leib Eisenberg

The German officer was furious. "I will not give you any other Jews to kill"—what impudence was this? How dare a Jew speak like that to a soldier of the German *Reich*? But he was not going to lose his self-control in front of a Jew. And so he, too, kept his own voice calm and even.

"I am afraid, my dear rabbi," he explained, "that I cannot accept your kind offer. I must reserve you for other purposes. We have special plans for you. I want two other Jews—not you, and not your wife. See that you have them ready for me no later than three days from now." With that, the German turned on his heel and left the rabbi's house.

The news of the Nazi commander's visit to the rabbi, and of the order he had given him, spread quickly among the Jews of Lask. But instead of surrendering to their despair, they became great with the spirit of holiness. This is what always happens; just as impurity and evil are contagious, so purity and saintliness have a way of spreading from one heart to another. And thus, when it became known that the saintly rabbi and his wife had offered to purchase the lives of two other Jews with their own, one Jew after the other came to the rabbi's house and said to him, "Rabbi, hand me over to the Germans so that I may die in your place and the rest of the community may live."

Altogether ten Jews offered their lives so that the rabbi, the rabbi's wife, and the others in the community might be spared. However, the rabbi stood firm. He refused to hand over any of his flock to the Nazis. The German commander was just as determined not to change his orders. The rabbi had refused to obey his command, and therefore had to be punished. But he was not to be allowed to die—just yet.

The German officer ordered all the Jews of Lask to gather in the market place, with their rabbi in the lead. When the Jews and the rabbi arrived at the market place, they found that they were surrounded by German soldiers. Standing some distance away was the entire Gentile population of the town, along with Gentiles from neighboring villages who had come to see what was going to happen to the Jews and the rabbi.

The German commander moved toward the rabbi. He raised his hand, and at his signal a priest appeared, bearing a huge crucifix. The priest planted the crucifix on the ground directly in front of the rabbi of Lask. The Nazi officer positioned himself next to the symbol of Christianity. "Kneel!" he shouted to the rabbi.

The Jews, the Gentiles and the Nazi soldiers watched in suspense. What would the rabbi do? Would he kneel before the crucifix? And if he did not, what would the Germans do to him?

The rabbi stepped forward; he seemed to be moving toward the crucifix. But then, with one sw..t ..ovement, he turned away from the crucifix and faced the German commander. He raised his right arm, and slapped the German full in the face—once, twice.

The others—Nazis, Christians and Jews—were frozen into stunned silence. The German commander was the first to come back to life. He made the one movement that seemed to come most naturally to a Nazi: he pulled his pistol from its holster.

The rabbi flung out his arms and presented his chest to the Nazi. "That's exactly what I wanted!" he cried. "Here! Shoot me!"

But the German commander had changed his mind. He did not want to do the rabbi the favor of shooting him on the spot. That would be much too good for a Jew. He was willing to swallow the insult which the Jew had dealt him in front of his own soldiers, because he wanted to think up a proper punishment for him—one infinitely more painful than swift death by a bullet aimed at his heart.

He ordered the rabbi to be taken away to the town jail, and commanded his soldiers to disperse the crowd. But everyone understood that this was not the end of the matter.

In his prison cell, the rabbi was told that the German commander had changed his plans and was going to do what he, the rabbi, had suggested in the first place just before the holiday of Purim: he was ordered to prepare to die on the gallows.

The German commander seemed to be spending an inordinate amount of time and effort in preparing for this hanging. He was deep in conferences with the hangman and with a team of German doctors. This was going to be a very special execution, said the German, licking his lips and rubbing his palms together in pure pleasure.

All the Gentiles of the town, and these Jews who were still left, were ordered to be present at the execution site. The rabbi calmly stepped toward the gallows and recited the confession of sins a Jew must make when he knows he is about to die. Calmly, he presented his head to the noose. The noose was tightened around his neck. The rabbi lost consciousness. But what was this? The hangman reached up and cut the noose! Then a German doctor came forward and bent over the unconscious figure on the ground. He was working to revive him! A murmur went through the crowd. What was this—a last-minute reprieve?

The German commander marched up to the gallows. "It is now eight o'clock!" he bellowed. "Everyone, including the rabbi, is to report at this site again three hours from now, at eleven o'clock sharp!"

Even the most hardened among the German soldiers were speechless with shock. It was incredible! The hangman had cut the noose just in time, and the doctor had revived the rabbi, not to restore him to life, but to keep him alive long enough to undergo a second hanging!

At eleven o'clock the procedure was exactly the same as it had been three hours earlier. The rabbi recited the confession of sins. The noose was placed around his neck and was tightened long enough for him to lose consciousness. Then the hangman cut the noose. The rabbi dropped to the ground, all but lifeless. Again, a German doctor came forward and revived him.

Again, the German commander was there, watching the scene. "Time out for lunch!" he shouted, almost jovially. "But I expect everyone, including the rabbi, to report back here at three o'clock! Remember—three o'clock sharp!

At three o'clock that afternoon, the rabbi was taken to the gallows for the third time. The noose was tightened and the rabbi became unconscious. Once again, the hangman cut the noose, just in time. But at this point there was a change in the procedure. This time the doctor who was ordered to revive the rabbi was not a German but a Jew. "Here's your rabbi," the German commander said. "Take him and work on him! He's all yours."

This time the Germans left the rabbi alone. More dead than alive, he was taken to the house of one of the town's Jews, where the doctor succeed in reviving him. Somehow, the doctor and the others managed to smuggle him out of Lask, and into the ghetto of the city of Lodz. There, one of the inmates, a surgeon, operated on him under the most primitive conditions imaginable to remove some fragmented bones from his neck. And by the grace of God, the rabbi recovered.

As soon as he was able to walk, he announced that he was leaving the ghetto and returning to Lask. The others begged him to remain in the ghetto. Here, no one knew him, and his anonymity might enable him to survive, whereas in Lask ... But the rabbi would not listen. "I am the rabbi of Lask," he said, "and a rabbi must not desert his community in the hour of need."

And so R. Judah Leib Eisenberg returned to Lask, and he was there when the Germans announced that the Jews of Lask would all be deported. Shoved aboard the truck that was to take him and the others on their last journey, he asked those near him to help him stand up. He was too weak to stand without assistance, he said with an apologetic smile, and he wanted to deliver one last sermon to his people.

The entire Jewish community of Lask was taken to the death camp of Chelmno. There, the rabbi, his wife, and most of the others, perished in the gas chambers. But miracles do happen and a few—a very few—of the Jews of Lask survived the Germans. After the war, these survivors learned that two of their rabbi's children were still alive, a daughter in New York and a son, David Eisenberg, in

Israel, where he had joined a group of Orthodox pioneers to rebuild the land. Each survivor remembered another passage from the sermon which the rabbi had preached on the truck that day on the way to Chelmno, and they repeated to the rabbi's children whatever portions they could recall.

From these passages, David Eisenberg, a talented writer, was able to reconstruct almost the entire sermon. Unfortunately, he, too, is now dead, and the manuscript was lost. Those who heard the rabbi speak and are still alive today have grown old and they no longer remember the rabbi's exact words. But they still insist that this last sermon was the best they had ever heard their rabbi deliver.

Translated and adapted by Gertrude Hirschler

2.

The Dignity of Martyrdom

The Proper Way to Die

The Final Sacrifice

Sabbath at the Edge of the Grave

Melavah Malkah at Auschwitz

The Last Songs of Praise

The Last Escape

"We Need His Kind"

The Children Speak

The Proper Way to Die

This is the story of Rabbi Zvi Michelson, one of Warsaw's oldest rabbis, who, at the age of 79, became one of the 700,000 Jews killed in the death camp of Treblinka.

Early in 1942 the Germans first began their systematic raids on the Warsaw ghetto, snatching Jewish men, women and children from the warrens in which they had been "resettled" and transporting them to the extermination camps.

In the very first of these raids the Germans, aided by Ukrainian soldiers, surrounded the house in which Rabbi Michelson lived, and shouted through their megaphones that all those inside were to come out into the courtyard. All the Jews in the building obeyed the German command — except for Rabbi Michelson, who refused to budge. Those who would remain in their rooms, he reasoned, would soon be rooted out by the German soldiers. Their travail would not last long; they would be gunned down on the spot, and their bodies would be flung out into the street. There, chances were that other Jews would find them, pile them upon the carts that creaked through the ghetto alleys to collect the dead, and bury them in accordance with Jewish law. Those who would go to the Germans in the courtyard, on the other hand, would be loaded by the storm troopers onto trucks and taken to the death camps. There they would die, too, but not without suffering. Even worse, from what the rabbi had heard, they would not be buried at all but cremated, in violation of the Torah. And so Rabbi Michelson prepared himself to meet death as he felt befitted a man of his age and tradition. He put on his phylacteries, draped his *tallith* around his spare body, bolted the door of his room and waited for the Germans to come.

But things did not happen the way the rabbi had expected. Yes, the Germans, accompanied by a Jewish ghetto policeman,* kicked open the door and burst into Rabbi Michelson's room. But when the storm troopers saw the old man with the long, flowing white beard standing upright before them, stern of countenance and draped from shoulders to feet in his snowy-white, silver-bordered prayer robe, they were immobilized by an awe, indeed a fear, such as they probably had never known before. Years later, the ghetto policeman, who survived the war, was to tell the end of the story. "Why, it's Moses himself!" the policeman heard one of the Germans mutter. With that, the German silently turned and led the others out of the room, slamming the door and leaving Rabbi Michelson untouched.

Alone in his little room, the rabbi could hear the babble of the crowd in the courtyard below, mingled with the raucous shouts of the German soldiers. From his tiny window, he could see the others from his house being shoved onto huge German army trucks. And a thought far more frightening than death came to Rabbi Michelson. True, he had been granted a miraculous reprieve. But for how long? When the Germans would recover from their surprise, they would return and shoot him. That is how he

* The ghetto policemen were tragic, controversial figures. In some instances the German authorities gave them special privileges, including better food than the other ghetto inmates. After the war, many of these individuals insisted that they had had no other alternative than to join the ghetto police, and that, in fact, they had succeeded in saving, or at least prolonging, the lives of many of their fellow Jews. Nevertheless, the stigma of "collaborator" was to haunt them for many years to come.

would die, and he would die alone. In effect, by refusing to leave his room he had run away like a coward; he had deserted his brethren. Which, he asked himself, was the proper alternative — to die alone, with the chance that he alone might be found by some survivors outside and given a proper Jewish burial, or to go out to his brethren and be with them on their last journey? Which was the proper way for him to die?

It did not take Rabbi Michelson more than a moment to make his decision. He turned from the window, adjusted his *tallith*, and strode from the room. With firm steps, he descended the stairs and marched out into the courtyard. There he joined the others on their way to the *Umschlagplatz*, the assembly point from where they all were taken to Treblinka. He remained a source of comfort and inspiration to his brethren, and when the end came, he shared their fate. He is among the millions who have no graves, but he has a lasting memorial in the annals of valor and uprightness.

— Based on Rachel Auerbach, B'hutzot Warsaw, Tel Aviv, Am Oved Publishers, 5714 (1953-54).

The Final Sacrifice

W hen R. Abraham Mordecai Maroko first came to the town of Widawa about a year before the war, he did not give the impression of a particularly spirited man. He was all skin and bones, and though he was only in his early twenties — he had married but a short time before — his skin was sallow and wrinkled, his back was bent, and he looked like a wizened old man.

After he had settled down in Widawa, however, he turned out to be a born leader. When he spoke, people forgot about his unprepossessing appearance and listened to him spellbound. He was able to put the know-it-alls in their places and succeeded in asserting his authority even over the kosher butchers of the village, who were known far and wide for their insolence. At the same time, Rabbi Maroko showed infinite compassion for the poor, the humble and the distressed.

Widawa was a hamlet somewhere between the cities of Wielun and Lodz, a Godforsaken cluster of straw-thatched shacks. But in a matter of months after his arrival, Rabbi Maroko had given the place a new lease on life. He set up charities, established a Talmud Torah for the small children and even founded a primary yeshiva for older boys. Before long, he had won not only the respect but also the genuine affection of the Jews in Widawa.

When the war broke out, most of the people of Widawa, notably the Jews, fled east, into the Russian-occupied part of Poland. The rumor spread that the final border between the German and Russian sectors of Poland would be, in fact, quite close to Widawa. The Warta river, just to the east of the village, would form the natural dividing line between the German and Russian forces. Only the sick, the old, and those too badly frightened to save themselves remained in Widawa.

There was one other person who refused to leave, though he was neither old, nor sick, nor frightened: R. Abraham Mordechai Maroko. His young wife pleaded with him: "Let us go away from here, Abraham Mordechai! The Germans are coming! Your life is in danger!"

But the rabbi replied: "If I leave, who will care for the old and the sick who will stay here because they cannot

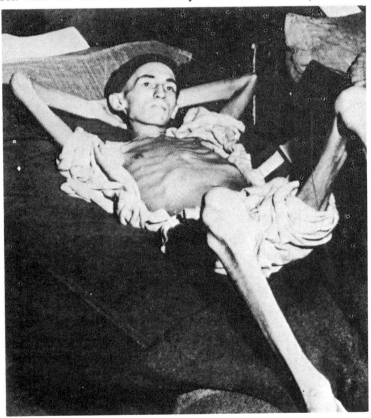

even leave their beds? As long as there are any Jews in this village, it is my duty to remain with them."

And so R. Abraham Mordechai Maroko stayed in Widawa and took care of the old and the sick who could not leave. Even after the German forces had entered the village, his resourcefulness enabled him to obtain the necessities of life for those still in Widawa.

So it continued until one warm fall day during the solemn season between Rosh HaShanah and Yom Kippur. The rabbi had retired to his room for a few hours of study, softly chanting the sacred text to himself. Suddenly he heard shouts in German outside: "Where does the Jew rabbi of this town live?"

At first no one answered. Those few Polish Gentiles who had remained in the village knew no German. But Bodnarek, the village cripple, understood just one word: *"Rabbiner."* He knew that this was the German name for the rabbi. So the Germans were looking for the rabbi of the filthy *zhids!* Well, Bodnarek exulted, this would be his great day. He was going to show everybody in the village tavern that Bodnarek the cripple was not the fool they all thought him to be. And so he hopped up and down on his good leg, pointed his thin crooked finger in the direction of the rabbi's house and shouted: "There! Over there! that's where the Jew *Rabbiner* lives!"

The Germans broke into the home of Rabbi Maroko, taunted him, beat him, and pulled at his beard and earlocks until his face was covered with blood. But then one of the soldiers noticed something interesting in the rabbi's room — a little box with a velvet curtain. He strode up to the box, flung the curtain aside and yanked out the Rabbi's Torah scroll. The others released the rabbi long enough to look at the strange object.

"Rabbi," said one of them, "would you care to explain to us just what this thing is?"

Rabbi Maroko proceeded to explain, in an old-fashioned, elegant German, what the "thing" was, and for what purpose the Jews used it. The soldiers waited for him to finish. Then the German who had discovered the scroll said:

"Come on, men, let's put on a little show! We'll have everybody in this place watch the rabbi set fire to that holy scroll of his!"

With that, the Germans threw the scroll to the rabbi, who caught it in his arms and hugged it tightly to him, not releasing it even when the Germans dragged him out of his house. Amidst kicks and slaps they pushed him into the village square, shouting: "Come one and all! Come and watch the rabbi perform!"

One of the Germans produced a can of gasoline, knocked the scroll from the Rabbi's hands and poured gasoline over the scroll. Then he handed the rabbi a lighted match.

"Here! Set that scroll on fire!"

A little crowd had gathered in the village square and looked on in a mixture of incomprehension and dumb fear. The rabbi no longer seemed small and round-shouldered.

"No! No!" he shouted. "Heaven forbid!" He bent and snatched up the scroll from the ground. "I will not burn the Law of God!"

In reply, the soldier picked up the gasoline can, poured the rest of its contents on the rabbi's head and set him afire along with his Torah scroll. Instantly a sheet of fire flared up and enveloped the rabbi. One of the villagers who witnessed the scene reported afterwards that the rabbi kept on reciting prayers at the top of his voice until he collapsed.

Thus did R. Abraham Mordechai Maroko make his final sacrifice and literally ascend to heaven in the midst of a pillar of fire.

Sabbath at the Edge of the Grave

Early one Friday morning in the spring of 1943 the Nazis herded together two dozen Jews from the town of Dombrowa and escorted them at gunpoint to the Jewish cemetery. Once they had arrived there, the Nazis handed the Jews spades and ordered them to dig a deep, wide ditch. They then commanded the Jews to line up in front of the ditch they had dug. All day long the Jews were forced to stand motionless before their own open mass grave, under the muzzles of the Nazi guns. But the Nazis seemed in no hurry to pull their triggers.

Among the Jews lined up before the open ditch was R. Hayyim Yehiel Rubin, the *rebbe* of Dombrowa. At

noontime, the *rebbe* noticed, standing aside, half-hidden behind a tree, a little old man. This was the gravedigger, whom the Nazis had apparently overlooked. The *rebbe* motioned to the man and asked him to go into town and bring back with him two loaves of bread. For all that the *rebbe* knew, they might still be standing before the Nazi guns when the Sabbath would arrive, and he, the *rebbe*, was determined to welcome the Sabbath properly.

As the day wore on, the *rebbe* became increasingly agitated. He had his Sabbath loaves now, but there was something else that troubled him deeply. This was the first Friday in his life as an adult Jew that he had not gone to the *mikvah* to purify his body in honor of the day of rest. And this had to happen now of all days, on this special Sabbath of Sabbaths, when he and his flock were about to meet their Father in Heaven face to face. How could he come before his Maker, on the Sabbath, in a state of impurity?

The sun had set, but the order to fire had not yet gone forth. "The Sabbath is about to begin," the *rebbe* said softly. "This is the last time we will greet the Sabbath on earth. My children, let us welcome this Sabbath with the same love that the Lord lavished upon us, His people, when He gave us the Sabbath to keep."

Having said this to his flock, he began to chant, ever so softly, the psalms with which Jews have ushered in the Sabbath from time immemorial. He did this while the Nazis kept their guns pointed at those Jews who insisted on singing the praises of their God even at the edge of their own open grave.

After completing his prayers, the *rebbe* bade "Good Sabbath" to the others and sang *Shalom Aleichem*, the hymn welcoming the angels of Sabbath peace into the Jewish home. The gravedigger, who survived to tell this story, had placed the loaves of bread upon the wet grass near the *rebbe*'s feet. The *rebbe* now turned and recited the *kiddush* over the bread. Then he launched into a learned discourse on the function of the 22 letters of the Hebrew alphabet in the Torah. But in the midst of his discourse, the *rebbe*, carried away by ecstasy, burst into joyous song. Those who stood on either side of him picked up the melody, and they all began to dance, there, before the mass grave that was waiting for them.

At that moment, the leader of the Nazi firing squad screamed, "Fire!" and so it was in the midst of a dance in praise of God and of His loving-kindness that the Jews from Dombrowa and their *rebbe* returned their souls to their Creator in complete purity.

— *Based on a report in the* Jewish Daily Forward, *March 3, 1946.*

Melaveh Malkah* At Auschwitz

What I am about to relate took place in Auschwitz, during the summer of 1944. One Sabbath I learned that we were going to have another "selection" — the standard Nazi procedure for supplying new "consignments" of inmates to feed the ovens. I was terror-stricken, but not for myself. I was working in the *Stubendienst*[8] and was therefore exempt from "selections." But I feared for the fate of my friends in the Hasidic group. I wondered which ones of them had already been taken from their barracks for the journey to the gas chambers.

That evening, after the Sabbath had ended, I went to the barracks where the young Hasidim used to meet. There, what I had feared all day became a sad certainty: I was told that the murderer Josef Mengele had come to the barracks and had been seen noting down the inmates' serial numbers. Everyone knew what that meant: those whose numbers had been taken would go to the gas chambers the next day.

But these young men, doomed to die though they were, showed spiritual strength beyond imagining. There were no tears, no sighs. In fact, my friends did not even seem particularly sad. They had resigned themselves to their fate, and now there were more important things to do. The Sabbath had to be seen out properly. The only food in the barrack was stale bread, but that did not keep the company from retelling the wisdom of the Sages and

---

* "Farewell to the Sabbath." A festive Saturday night meal, accompanied by singing and dancing, to "see the Sabbath out."

singing Hasidic tunes to speed the Sabbath Queen on her way. My friend Nahum Halter of Lubatov, Volhynia, belted out a lively Hasidic marching song, and all the others joined in.

Everyone performed the ritual washing of hands and ate a *kezayit** of bread to fulfill the commandment of bidding farewell to the Sabbath with a meal. One of the men — I think his name was Naftali Werdyger — recited a saying of the famed R. Simha Bunim of Przysucha.[9]

"Said Rabbi Simha Bunim of Przysucha: When I will arrive in the world to come and I will be asked, 'What did you do on your last night on earth, Bunim?' I will answer, 'I took part in a meal of brotherhood.' "

"From this," said Naftali Werdyger, "you can see how important it is for Hasidim to eat, sing and study together as brothers, even as we do tonight."

And this is how, with words of Torah and songs of *Hasidut* on their lips, these young men spent their last night on earth.

— *Based on account by Leibel Bornstein, of Lodz, who survived Auschwitz and settled in Zurich after the war.*

---

* Quantity the size of an olive; the minimum quantity of food over which a following blessing may be recited.

The Last Songs of Praise

On June 3, 1941, two days after the outbreak of the war between Germany and the Soviet Union, some 3,000 Jews from the Galician town of Zloczow were arrested and the old synagogue was set on fire. In the last minute the Jews managed to rescue the Torah scrolls from the burning synagogue. The Nazis herded all the Jews together and marched them to a place beyond the town limits. The procession was led by the elders of the community, each wrapped in his prayer shawl and carrying one of the scrolls from the synagogue. At the head of the elders was R. Meir Ofen, an aged Kabbalist who had lived in Rzeszow before the war. And they all chanted, "Rejoice in the Lord, O ye righteous" as they marched to the mass graves where the Nazi firing squads were waiting for them.[10]

One cold, dark winter night, the Germans discovered four elderly Jews who had hidden out somewhere in the town of Lutzk. They were the last Jews left in Lutzk; all the others had been deported or killed long before. Wrapped in filthy tatters, their beards unkempt, these four Jews had between them only one possession to carry: a Torah scroll. Now they were being led to the gallows by the Germans, followed by a drunk, jeering mob of Poles and Ukrainians. One of the Germans beat out a ceaseless tattoo on his drum.

When the group arrived at the hanging site, one of the Nazis shouted: "Come on, Jews, let's dance a little!" And the four Jews began to move to the rhythm of the

THE UNCONQUERABLE SPIRIT

drumbeat. Once again the German rapped out an order: 'Now sing something!' And the Jew who held the Torah scroll in his arms began to sing in a loud, firm voice, truly with the last of his strength, "You must know that the Lord is God — He was, He is and He shall be forevermore." He sang this to the tune used in the synagogue on the holiday of *Simhat Torah*, the Rejoicing over the Law of God.[11]

The Last Escape

O n August 12, 1942, German troops occupied the town
of Korczyna=Korczin in the Russian-held sector of
Poland and drove all the Jews from their homes into the
town square. Only Wolf Kirschner and his twelve-year-
old son David Leib managed to elude the Germans by es-
caping through the rear door of their house. Under cover
of darkness, father and son fled to the Jewish cemetery,
where they hid out all night long.

The next morning, Wolf Kirschner learned that the
town had been pounded into rubble and that all the Jews
had been taken away in German army trucks. He realized
that he and his son were, in effect, trapped. Death was
sure. And at this point Wolf Kirschner made a decision
born of despair — and courage. Rather than be deported
by the Germans, he and his son would meet death in the
Jewish cemetery, among the graves of their own people.

Wolf went to the keeper of the cemetery, a Gentile.
Handing him some money, he asked the Pole to dig a
grave next to the place where his father, Michael
Kirschner, lay buried. Then he told the cemetery keeper to
call the Polish town police.

When the policemen arrived at the cemetery, Wolf
Kirschner and his son climbed into the newly-dug grave,
and the policemen shot them.

Thus the two last surviving Jews of Korczyna
escaped deportation and came to rest in holy ground
among their fathers.

A year after the war, Wolf Kirschner's sister-in-law, who had found a new home in Canada, sent money to the cemetery keeper to have a monument erected at the grave of the father and the son. The Polish inscription on the monument reads:

Here lie Wolf Kirschner and his son David Leib, who perished at the hands of the Hitlerite murderers on August 15, 1942, in Korczyna.

— Based on account by Itzhak Englard-Wasserstrom
in Korcziner Yiskor-Bukh.

"We Need His Kind"

by L. Feingold

I was taken from the Warsaw ghetto to the death camp of Treblinka in 1942. With me on that day at the Warsaw railroad siding, where the boxcars were waiting to receive us, stood two patriarchal figures: the writer and philosopher Hillel Zeitlin[12] and Rabbi Isaac Meir Kanal, who was the *rebbe* of Blaszko and a member of the Warsaw Rabbinical Court.

"I will not enter this train," Rabbi Kanal declared. "I would rather be killed here, in Warsaw. Then at least my body will be put into the ground as our Law demands.

Where they want to take us, there will be no graves — only ovens."

At first Zeitlin listened quietly. He gnawed nervously at the tuft of hair beneath his lower lip. His large eyes protruded from their sockets and seemed to grow larger still. He appeared to be deep in thought. With his right hand he reached into the bundle which he held clutched under his left arm and which contained his most precious possessions — his books and his *tallith*. Quickly, he pulled out his *tallith* and flung it around his shoulders. Then, in a low but firm voice, he began to speak:

"Fellow Jews, I am sorry that I do not have any poison tablets with me. Under ordinary circumstances one who takes his own life forfeits his portion in the world to come. But if one is helpless and in danger of falling into the hands of criminals, it is permissible to die by one's own hand. Of such Jews it has been said that they, too, are deserving of eternal life. But then, unfortunately, as I have just told you, I did not come prepared. But you, fellow Jews, are in a better position than I. You are still young and strong. Don't go to your death without a fight! I am old and broken. I have no way of ending my life, nor am I strong enough to use my fists against these murderers. You, on the other hand, are free to choose: If you will it, you can glorify the Name of God by your actions for all to see. You will die no matter what you will do. But you must not die like cats or dogs. Go to your death with your heads held high, as proud men and Jews. Do not allow that scum to violate the image of God in which you were created. If you must die, take some of the murderers with you! Fight them! With your bare fists, if need be!"

Those who heard these words were shaken to the very depth of their souls. Then they sprang to life and struck out at their German tormentors with their bare

Rabbi Isaac Meir Kanal

fists. Captain Schmerling, the SS officer in command of the deportation train, was beaten until he bled and could not walk. (He lived to be "liquidated" by the Polish underground).

At this point the Polish police opened fire on us and, in the ensuing panic, the SS men, helped by their Ukrainian and Lithuanian underlings, fell upon the Jews, kicking and shoving them into the boxcars.

But Rabbi Kanal was still standing at the door of the boxcar. He refused to move from the spot, blocking the way of the others. He was shouting so loudly that an SS man nearby — his name was Hantke — held his hands over his ears to drown out the sound.

"Beat me! Kill me! I won't go! I want to die here! Not in the ovens!"

At that moment Rabbi Kanal, Zeitlin and I were lifted bodily from the platform into the boxcar. Wedged in between us was Reb Mendele Alter of Pabianice, president of the Polish Union of Orthodox Rabbis and brother of the Gerer *rebbe*. The door of the boxcar thumped shut, sealing us off from the world outside. But minutes later, the door creaked open again. Before us, on the platform below, in the bright sunlight, stood two members of the *Judenrat* — Kahn and Heller. Close behind them were two SS men — Hantke, who had been so unnerved by Rabbi Kanal's shouts only minutes before, and another officer, whose name was Brand. Heller was shouting in a mixture of Yiddish and German:

"Rabbi Mendele of Pabianice! Will Rabbi Mendele Alter come to the door of the car!"

We were thunderstruck. Heller was going to remove Reb Mendele from the death train! He was going to save Reb Mendele! Had he made a deal with the Nazis for the life of this one Jew?

"Here I am!" came Reb Mendele's reply. His voice was thin, barely audible. "I'm coming! Just a minute! It's hard to move here — so crowded! One moment, please! I'm coming!"

Meanwhile, Brand was using his whip right and left. Reb Mendele was distraught.

"Oh! Oh!" he moaned. "Don't beat these poor Jews on my account! Stop it! I'm coming! Let me through!

Reb Mendele Alter

Please! Please! I'm coming! Just stop beating these poor people!"

Clearly Reb Mendele, that saintly man, had no idea why he was being singled out from the others.

At last, Reb Mendele reached the door of the boxcar. He was deathly pale and tears were coursing down his cheeks.

Kahn, the *Judenrat* representative, moved toward him. "Please!" he said quietly. "Make way! We're trying to get this man off the train!" He lifted his arms and held them out to Reb Mendele. But SS officer Brand pulled Kahn back.

"No!" he shouted. "I've changed my mind. You can't take this man off the train! We need his kind in Treblinka."

— Based on L. Feingold's article in HaTzofeh,
Nisan 27, 1946.

The Children Speak

Every Sabbath morning, those Jews who were still left in the Galician town of Sokol gathered at the home of their *rebbe* to hold services. On Saturday, August 15, 1942, the Gestapo raided the *rebbe's* house and arrested the worshippers — 31 in all, including the *rebbe's* young son. Still wearing their prayer shawls, the Jews were herded onto trucks and driven to Gestapo headquarters. There, they all were shot.

After the war, a Ukrainian police officer related what he had seen and heard at Gestapo headquarters that day. The *rebbe's* young son looked the Nazi hangman straight in the eye and said to him, "If you kill us, all the German people will pay for it! You'll see! Your end is near!" In answer, the German seized a hatchet and struck the boy down with one blow.[13]

All the Jews of the town of Linovice were taken to the cemetery together. Marching at the head of his flock was Rabbi Ahrele Rabin, garbed in his white shroud, held in at the waist by a wide belt. The youngest in the procession was a small boy, who is remembered today only by his first name and the first name of his mother — Ephraim, son of Hannah.

As they neared the cemetery, the rabbi said to his congregation:

"My dear brethren, after all the hellish pain we have endured in this world, we are about to enter the Kingdom of Heaven. I can assure you that you will all go directly to Paradise. Therefore do not be afraid; rather, go forth in joy to meet your fate. Fortunate you, fortunate we, that we have been found worthy of the privilege of dying as Jews. Our only crime was that we are Jews, and this is why we are about to leave this life. Therefore, let us go with a quiet heart. We will march straight to that place where rest the righteous for whose sake God has permitted the world to endure."

Before the Ukrainian guards were able to make a move, little Ephraim walked up to the rabbi, took hold of his wide belt and began to cry. "Rabbi," he sobbed, "Please don't leave me! Let me hold your hand so it won't be so hard to die!"

And so the Jews of Linovice, led by their rabbi and a little child, entered the cemetery. There, they were all shot and buried together in one mass grave.[14]

3.

How They Kept The Law of God

THE UNCONQUERABLE SPIRIT

The Torah in the Ghetto

The Torah tells us, "You shall therefore keep My statutes, and My ordinances, which, if a man do, he shall live by them." [15] Our Sages interpret "he shall live by them" to mean that it is not the Torah's intent that anyone should die as a result of observing the Law of God. [16] The Sabbath, the dietary laws, even the fast of Yom Kippur, may be broken to save a human life.

Among the few documents that have survived from the ghetto of Lodz there is one which mirrors both the tragedy of ghetto life and the spiritual greatness of the Torah scholars during the era of the Nazi Holocaust. It demonstrates that the rabbis never dealt lightly with questions of religious observance, not even in the starving, disease-ridden ghettoes of Nazi-occupied Poland. But at the same time it shows the loving concern of these teachers of the Law for the life and well-being of all their fellow Jews, a concern so great that they felt constrained to hand down an official ruling to define the circumstances under which non-kosher meat might be eaten by Jews in the ghetto in order to prevent death from starvation or malnutrition.

O f all the signatories to the above document, the last to
survive in the ghetto of Lodz was Rabbi Joseph ("Reb
Yossele") Feiner, one of the outstanding Orthodox rabbis
in Poland. He had been a favorite student of one of the
great Torah authorities of pre-war Eastern Europe, Rabbi
Eliezer Wachs of Kalisz.

"During most of the year that I spent in the ghetto of
Lodz," a survivor relates, "I was locked up in the ghetto
prison along with others who, like myself, had been sent
back from the forced labor camps as *unproductive* individuals. Only for a month and a half was I out of jail
and free to move about within the ghetto. On one Sabbath
during my *free* period I paid a visit to Reb Yossele Feiner,
who had been born in Piotrkov and had been a close
friend of my grandfather, Arye Eybeschuetz.

"Reb Yossele was then living on *Jew Street*, in a

thereafter consult the Rabbinate (at the Rabbinate Office, No. 4 Miodowa Street between noon and 3 P.M.) or any other individual rabbi, for instructions.

3. In addition to the foregoing, we hereby request the esteemed Chairman [*Judenalteste* Chaim M. Rumkowski] to instruct the respected medical authorities as to the great significance of rulings of this type, which should be pronounced only in cases involving actual danger to the life of the individual concerned.

Respectfully submitted,

[Rabbis] Joseph Feiner, Eliezer Lipschutz, Zelig Rothstein, Moses Weiss, Abraham Silman, Samuel David Lasky, Johanan Lipschutz, Aaron Bornstein, Akiva Eger, Eliahu Fleischaker, Simha Bunim Oberbaum, Nehemiah Alter, Shelomo Jacobovitz, Moses David Domb, Herschel Fischof.

* "Elder of the Jews." The head of the Jewish community.

small, dark room facing an inner courtyard. Before the war, he had been an imposing figure of patriarchal mein, with a snow-white, neatly trimmed beard. Now he sat before me, a bent old man, shorn of his beard, broken and crushed. But he greeted me warmly and for a few moments he was again the smiling, clear-eyed sage I had known once upon a time. Soon, however, he lapsed once more into silent brooding.

"After a while, we began to exchange reminiscences of days long past. Neither one of us had any illusions of what the future would hold, but Reb Yossele, that noble soul, tried his best to comfort me and to give me new courage."

After the war, survivors of the Lodz ghetto recalled how Reb Yossele's own courage had not forsaken him until the end. They told of many instances in which Reb Yossele, sometimes at the risk of his own life, was able to persuade the *Judenalteste*, Chaim M. Rumkowski, to desist from some particularly degrading act in which he had been ready to collaborate at the behest of the Nazi authorities.

(It should be added here, however, that Rumkowski in the end demonstrated his loyalty to his people. When the Lodz ghetto was liquidated in August, 1944, he and his family voluntarily joined the last transport of ghetto inmates to Auschwitz, where he was killed.)[17]

As the Passover season of 1943 approached, the religious leaders of the Warsaw ghetto community were aware that the ghetto would soon rise in full-scale revolt against the German overlords. Accordingly, the rabbis were concerned that their congregants should maintain their health as much as possible in order to be fit for the ordeal that lay ahead. They therefore ruled that on this Passover, legumes — peas, beans and lentils, all of them starchy vegetables — might be eaten. This ruling was upheld even by such zealous spiritual leaders as the Tzaddik of Piaseczno, whose entire community had been uprooted from its original home and interned in the Warsaw ghetto two years before.

But when it came to laws and customs that could be observed without detriment to health and strength, the rabbis of the Warsaw ghetto remained firm. Thus, shortly before Passover that year, a request was received from the *rebbe* of Kuziglov to make a chemical test of the margarine rations that were being distributed in the ghetto. The *rebbe* wanted to make sure that the margarine did not contain any non-kosher fat.

On the day before Passover, Rabbi Benjamin Morgenstern, *rebbe* of Sokolow Podlaski, raised yet another question. The time had come for the Jews to sell whatever *hametz* they still had in their homes. But since Polish Gentiles hardly ever entered the ghetto, there was no Gentile to whom the *hametz* could be sold. Since the food was far too scarce and costly to be thrown out before Passover, it was vitally important to carry out this piece of legal fiction. A way was finally found.

The *rebbe* learned that a wagon driver named Stanski came regularly to the ghetto to remove junk and refuse. He contacted Stanski, and the Pole promptly agreed to act as the "purchaser" in the deed of sale — for a handsome cash reward, of course.[18]

Rabbi Shmuel David Ungar

He Stood Firm:
The Story of
Rabbi Samuel David Ungar of Nitra

Before the war, the town of Nitra in Slovakia had been a bastion of Jewish tradition and learning. Its Yeshiva had a name throughout the world of Orthodox Jewry, drawing students from the Hasidic East as well as from the modern West. The Yeshiva and the community of Nitra were led by the saintly Rabbi Samuel David Ungar. Even before coming to Nitra, Rabbi Ungar had been known as a great teacher and moralist far beyond the borders of Slovakia. Only two years before the outbreak of the war, he had been elected by the Agudath Israel, the world organization of Orthodox Jewry, to its supreme religious body, the *Mo'etzet Gedolei HaTorah*, the international council of Torah sages.

Deportation of Jews from Nitra had begun as early as 1942, but during the two years that followed, the town was considered a relatively safe place for Jews, so that Jews from many other Slovak towns and villages took refuge there, hoping to be spared from deportation and death.

By early 1944, however, the deportation scheme was in full swing. That summer, hundreds of Jews left Nitra and went into hiding in the surrounding countryside where partisan units were harassing the Fascist overlords. Among those who fled to the woods around Nitra was Rabbi Samuel David Ungar.

All his life, Rabbi Ungar had been known for his uncompromising piety, his meticulous observance of the Law down to the last detail. He was not about to change now, not even when he was forced to live in the woods as a fugitive from the Slovak murderers. When the partisans offered him crusts of bread, he thanked them, but would not eat the bread; he had never partaken of bread baked in the ovens of non-Jews, and he was not going to begin doing so now. Sometimes partisans managed to obtain milk from nearby farmers, but Rabbi Ungar would not drink the milk because of the Talmudic prohibition against drinking milk taken from Gentile farms without the surveillance of a Jew: the milk might not come from a cow but from some forbidden animal. He would not even boil potatoes because the precious water had to be saved for the daily ritual washing of hands: a Jew could not move four cubits from his bedstead in the morning without first cleansing his hands with water. Most of all, he worried about the approaching fall holidays, because he would not be able to get a *shofar*. How would he carry out the commandment bidding every Jew to hear the blast of the ram's horn on Rosh HaShanah?

As the weeks went by, the rabbi steadily lost flesh and strength. One day a friend brought him some grapes — only heaven knows from where — and pleaded with him to eat them. But Rabbi Ungar was firm: he could not eat these grapes. He would have to save them for making wine. A Jew had no right to enjoy grapes as long as he had no wine with which to sanctify the next Sabbath.

As fall turned into winter, Rabbi Ungar failed rapidly. He was no longer young; his sixtieth birthday was not far off. But despite the heavy snow and the bitter cold, he spent a few hours in the middle of each day huddled at the opening of his bunker in order to study, by the pale winter light, the holy books he had taken with him into hiding.

Rabbi Michael Ber Weissmandl

Rabbi Ungar died in the woods from starvation and exposure only weeks before the fall of the Third Reich. He was buried in the Jewish cemetery of Piestany next to his father, who had been the rabbi of that town.

Rabbi Ungar's son, Rabbi Solomon Ungar, and his son-in-law, Rabbi Michael Ber Weissmandl,* survived the

---

* The story of Rabbi Weissmandl represents an epic in its own right. A brilliant young Talmudic scholar, Rabbi Weissmandl proved also adept in the practical work of helping organize an "underground railroad" by way of which Polish Jews were moved to Slovakia and from there to still-neutral Hungary. When the Germans began their planned

war and settled in the United States. There, with help from American Jews, including former students of the Yeshiva of Nitra, the two refugee scholars built up a new Nitra Yeshiva at Mount Kisco, amidst the hills of New York's Westchester County. Rabbi Weissmandl planned the new Yeshiva as an institution where, in addition to Talmudic training, the students would acquire skills in farm work and in such trades as printing. Unfortunately, it was not given to Rabbi Weissmandl to see the fulfillment of his dream. His health broken by the years of war and persecution, he died in 1958.

— *Based on articles by Zvi Jacob Abraham, in* Eleh Ezkerah, *Vol.II, pp. 251-64, New York, 5717 (1956-7), and on "The History of Agudath Israel in Slovakia (1918-39)" by Gertrude Hirschler, in* The Jews of Czechoslovakia, *Vol.II, Philadelphia, 1971, pp.155-72.*

program of mass deportations, he joined with Mrs. Gisi Fleischmann, a Zionist leader, to head the "Working Group," an organized effort to rescue Jews regardless of ideological or religious affiliation. The "Working Group" managed to transmit messages to Jews in the still-free countries of Europe and America, informing them of what was about to happen and urging them to act to avert disaster. Thanks to the efforts of the "Working Group," deportations from Slovakia were actually stopped for a time in 1942, allowing a large number of Jews to find shelter in places where they survived the war. Rabbi Weissmandl himself lost his wife and children in the Holocaust, but remarried and started a new family in the United States.

The Last Seder of
R. Menahem Zemba

*Rabbi Menahem Zemba was born in Praga,
Poland in 1883, the son of a poor Hasidic family. While still a young man, he became well
known for his Talmudic erudition. Thanks to
financial support from his wealthy father-in-
law, he was able to devote all his time to rabbinical studies for a period of 20 years. In 1935
he became a member of Warsaw's Council of
Rabbis and for a time served as secretary of the
Mo'etzet Gedolei HaTorah, the international
council of Torah sages.*

*Rabbi Zemba was one of the last rabbis to
remain in the Warsaw ghetto. On January 14,
1943, at a meeting of rabbis and other communal leaders in the ghetto, he gave his rabbinic
endorsement for the planned Warsaw ghetto
uprising. In his view, the hour demanded more
than passive martyrdom without a fight. He
said:*

*"In the past, during times of religious
persecution, Jewish law required that we give
up our lives, even for the least essential practice.
But now, when we are faced by an archenemy
whose unparalleled ruthlessness and program
of total annihilation knows no bounds, the Law
demands that we fight and offer resistance to*

the very end, with unequaled determination and valor in order to sanctify the name of God."

Rabbi Zemba refused an offer from the Catholic clergy to help him escape from the ghetto. He was killed by the Nazis on the fifth day of the revolt. His life's work, a manuscript of over 3,000 pages on Maimonides, was lost in the ghetto. The story of Rabbi Zemba's last days is told by his nephew, who survived the war.

E arly in April, 1943 the word spread through the Warsaw ghetto that SS *Reichsfuhrer* Heinrich Himmler himself had visited Warsaw and given orders that the city should be made *judenrein* as a present to Adolf Hitler on his birthday, April 20. No one thought to question the rumor; the very air of the ghetto was heavy with the approaching storm.

The time for making plans was long past. Every Jew in the Warsaw ghetto had made his own personal decision: to attempt to escape from the ghetto into the Aryan sector of the city, or to remain and hide out, or to remain and fight the enemy. Meanwhile, the Nazis were laying their plans for the extermination of what was left of Warsaw's Jewish community. They knew that this would not be an easy task; they had received reports that the Jews in the ghetto were arming and preparing to offer stiff resistance. Accordingly, they made some modifications in their strategy. They would try to achieve their ends by friendly persuasion. Toebbens and Schultz, the two Nazis who directed the ghetto's leather workshops and so were in close touch with thousands of ghetto inmates, were named to the newly-created post of ghetto commissars. Their orders were to keep the Jews calm and to start a propaganda campaign urging the Jews to move with their workshops out of the crowded ghetto and into the labor camps that had been built especially for them near Lublin.

But the Jews of the Warsaw ghetto were not taken in by the blandishments of Toebbens and Schultz. The "party" — as the ghetto resistance movement had become known — immediately launched a counter-propaganda drive, complete with posters and secretly circulated handbills, warning the Jews not to permit themselves to be fooled by the Germans.

As the mood of suspense and apprehension mounted in the ghetto, the home of my uncle, Rabbi Menahem Zemba, became a source of solace and new hope for thousands of Jews who flocked there to seek the rabbi's counsel. Rabbi Zemba listened patiently to everyone who came to seek his for advice. He urged all those who could possibly do so to escape into the Aryan sector beyond the ghetto walls. Those unable to leave the ghetto, he said, should find hiding places for themselves in basements or attics. But no matter what their decision, they were not to follow the suggestion of the Germans to move to Lublin, for that would be suicide.

Yet, when a delegation representing thousands of Jews employed in the ghetto workshops called on him and asked him whether they should agree to move to the labor camps, Rabbi Zemba hesitated to assume sole responsibility for their fate. He called a meeting of the ghetto's remaining rabbis and communal leaders to discuss the question. At this meeting he repeated his personal conviction that the Jews of Warsaw should not let themselves be misled by the Germans. When one of the participants in the discussion ventured the opinion that caution was in order when it came to disseminating such a categorical view, Rabbi Zemba replied that he considered it his duty to warn his community of the Nazi trap.

Some heartrending scenes took place at the rabbi's apartment. One day a young couple appeared, both of them in tears. The husband wanted to give his wife a divorce. No, they were not unhappy together; the problem was something else. The husband had an opportunity to smuggle himself out of the ghetto into the Aryan sector and, naturally, had wanted to take his wife with him. But the young woman was afraid that her pronounced Jewish features would give them both away. Besides, her parents were in the ghetto and she did not want to abandon them to almost certain death. But she did not want her husband to lose his chance to escape because of her. At first, her husband had refused to leave the ghetto without her. Finally, however, he had acceded to her tearful pleas that he save himself, but only under the condition that they first go to the rabbi and obtain a divorce. If they were to be separated, he pointed out to his shocked wife, and he were to be killed, she probably would have no way of establishing beyond all doubt that he was not, in fact, alive somewhere. In that case, under Jewish law, if she survived she would remain forever an *agunah*, neither wife nor widow, unable to rebuild her life in a new marriage. By divorcing her before he left the ghetto, her husband wanted to protect her from that tragic fate. If she would not consent to the divorce, he would not leave her. Rabbi Zemba understood only too well what he had to do. With tears streaming down his cheeks, he wrote out the bill of divorcement.

A young man, accompanied by his aged mother, came to Rabbi Zemba with a strange request. He wanted the rabbi to persuade his mother to undergo baptism. The young man had been assigned to a labor detail outside the ghetto. There, he had met a Polish gentile who had offered to hide him and his mother at his home. The Gentile wanted to be paid, of course, but that was not the main difficulty. The problem was much more delicate than that. It had occurred to the Gentile, a devout Catholic, that it would be a sin for him to give shelter to Jews. He had therefore informed the young man that he would be able in good conscience to save him and his mother from the Nazis only if both of them would agree to be baptized in the Catholic Church. The young man was ready to take that step in order to remain alive, but the old woman cried bitterly, sobbing that she would rather die as a Jewess than live as a gentile. Her son argued that in times such as these, anything was permitted if it offered a chance of survival. But Rabbi Zemba said to him: "Your mother says she wants to remain alive only if she can live as a Jewess. Do you really expect me, then, to tell her to end her days as a gentile?"

Meanwhile, the dreaded date — April 20 — was drawing closer. About three weeks before Passover, Rabbi Zemba called another meeting of rabbis. Among those who attended were Rabbi Goldschlag of Sherpetz, Rabbi Landa of Kolobiel, the rabbi of Wolle, Rabbi Beer, and Rabbi Eliezer Itche Meisels, grandson of the renowned Rabbi of Lodz. They decided to proclaim the day before the New Moon of Nisan as a day of repentance, prayer and charity to avert the fate that threatened the Jews of the Warsaw ghetto. On that day, the Jews were to fast in repentance of past misdeeds, to read a prayer composed by the rabbis especially for the occasion, and to donate money to the community so that no Jew in the ghetto would be prevented to buy Passover foods because he could not afford them.

Of course there was no way of making the rabbis' decision public, but the word spread quickly through the ghetto. On the day before the beginning of the Passover month, Jews throughout the ghetto gathered in back rooms and basements to offer their prayers. The apartment of Rabbi Zemba was filled almost to bursting with men and women who wept and prayed in a desperate plea for Divine mercy. I had heard my uncle preach many times before, but never had I heard him deliver such a soul-stirring appeal to hearts and minds as he did on that day.

He urged us all to have faith and not to give way to despair. As his text, he chose the last verse of Psalm 1: "For the Lord knows the way of the righteous, and the way of the lawless shall perish," and gave his own interpretation of the original verse to meet the need of the hour. "The way of the righteous," he explained, "is to know the Lord, to understand that His ways are perfect. The Master of the Universe knows what He is doing. It is only right, therefore, that we should put our trust in Him. To give up hope, to insist that all is lost, that we are doomed to perish — that would be the way of the lawless. The greatest sin of all is to cease trusting in the Lord. The preachers of despair are twice guilty: By spreading the message of despondency, they not only sin themselves but cause others to sin as well. Therefore, do not say, 'We shall perish' but 'We know that the ways of the Lord are just and righteous altogether.' "

During the weeks that followed, Rabbi Zemba demonstrated to us by his own example how we should show our trust in God and at the same time serve notice on our foes that we were not about to surrender. We were to be prepared for all eventualities, but even as we made our plans for the hour of decision, we were to carry on a normal life as a community of proud Jews, observing the Law of God. Passover was approaching and Jews needed matzoth, wine, and other foods with which to observe the holiday properly. Rabbi Zemba appointed a special Passover committee consisting of three outstanding communal leaders: Jacob Trockenheim, who before the war had been a wealthy industrialist and a member of the Polish Senate; Joseph Koenigsberg, who had been a prosperous manufacturer and president of the Yeshiva of Lublin, and Eliezer Gershon Friedenson, former editor of the *Beth Jacob Journal* and member of Warsaw's Jewish Community Council. Under the most adverse conditions imaginable, these men labored selflessly to procure Passover foods and make them available to as many Jews as possible. The apartment of Rabbi Joshua Perlow,* the Novominsker Rav, directly across the street from Rabbi Zemba's house on Kupiecka 7, was converted into a depot for Passover foods. All day long, crowds streamed into the building with scrips to pay for the wine and matzoth, and emerged with their bags filled. Despite the constant undercurrent of uncertainty and apprehension, the ghetto seemed to be taking on a holiday mood.

Then, on the day before the first Seder, the suspense broke. A Polish policeman spread a rumor that the Polish police had received orders from the Germans to take up stations at the ghetto walls at midnight. Everyone understood what that meant. The people vanished from the streets into their homes, gathering their last possessions for the move to their hideouts. Meanwhile, the members of the resistance movement made their final preparations for the confrontation with the enemy. They stationed men

---

* His brother, R. Nahum Perlow, was to survive the war and settle in Brooklyn, where he died at an advanced age in 1976.

at various strategic points and sent others on reconnaissance errands. Members of the underground also circulated among the workers in the ghetto workshops, keeping them informed of the latest developments but at the same time doing everything possible to allay fears and to prevent the outbreak of panic.

At ten o'clock that night the Jewish underground learned from reliable channels that the rumors about the impending German occupation of the ghetto were true. Within minutes, couriers were on the way to pass the word to the people in the workshops and the ghetto dwellings.

By midnight all the members of the Jewish resistance had taken up their battle stations. Almost every roof in the ghetto was manned, mostly by young boys who had never even come within touching distance of a rifle before but who were now as calm and ready for battle as seasoned veterans. They had vowed to themselves not to go to their deaths without a fight. If all hope of survival were to vanish, they would kill as many of the Nazi murderers as they could before using the last bullet to end their own lives. On second thought, they said, even that final bullet should not be squandered; it, too, could serve to put a Nazi out of the world. For themselves, they could always swallow a dose of potassium cyanide if all else failed. Almost everyone in the ghetto had managed to obtain enough of the poison for personal use if and when circumstances would demand it. The young men bade farewell to their loved ones. Not a word was uttered; only eyes met in silent leavetaking. The young men did not weep. They gritted their teeth and climbed to the rooftops with firm steps. Some carried revolvers or machine guns, others were armed with homemade Molotov cocktails, and those who could find no other weapons took with them bottles of acid and even toy pistols to fend off the enemy.

During the early hours of Passover eve, the first Nazi

detachments marched into the ghetto. They were met by a hail of gunfire from rooftops and hideouts. Momentarily caught off balance, they withdrew to regroup their forces. Thus began the battle of the Warsaw ghetto.

As one of the central figures in the ghetto, Rabbi Zemba had been the object of constant surveillance from the Germans. As a consequence, he had not been able to participate directly in the preparations for the battle. But his chief lieutenant, Joseph Koenigsberg, had served as one of the principal advisors of the resistance movement, and when the movement had launched a drive to raise funds for arms, Rabbi Zemba had been one of the first contributors. For months, the attic of Kupiecka 7 had been used by the Jewish resistance movement as a hideout and observation point. Now, it was to serve as a shelter for Rabbi Zemba.

The battle raged all that day. Gunfire was met by gunfire and the ghetto resounded with the noises of war. Again and again, the Germans tried to force their way into the ghetto, but each time they were compelled to retreat.

Rabbi Zemba found himself sharing his shelter with about 100 others, men and women, representing every segment of the ghetto population. With some of them, the rabbi had little, if anything, in common. But this did not trouble him. He was sufficient company unto himself — or perhaps he sensed the presence of another, higher Being. Only when I observed him there in the packed attic did I understand what he had once said to me when I expressed my resentment at seeing a well-known member of the Jewish community taking up his precious time with trivialities. I had marveled at my uncle's patience, but he had replied, "God, praise be to Him, gave me a very healthy mind. If I talk with someone and he begins to bore me, I am able to pursue my own thoughts even while I listen to him." So, too, it was now, on the eve of Passover in the Warsaw ghetto. The attic hideout was filled with all manner of people, but Rabbi Zemba was able to preserve his spiritual privacy.

Night fell. The Passover holiday had begun. The rabbi glanced at his watch and asked whether everyone in the attic had with him his personal portion of matzoth required for the observance of the Seder. Already weeks before, he had prepared for himself matzoth small enough to keep in his coat pocket at all times and had urged everyone else to do likewise. "We don't know where we will be when Passover comes," he had said. "But if we keep some matzoth with us wherever we go, we will be able at least to observe the precept of eating matzoth on the Seder nights no matter where we go."

At long last, there was a lull in the shooting outside. The rabbi led us down the steps into his apartment to celebrate the Seder. He recited the Haggadah with unusual devotion, frequently interspersing the traditional text with profound, erudite comments of his own.

During the early hours of the next morning, the first day of Passover, the Nazis, now supported by additional troops and tank divisions, succeeded in breaking into the ghetto. Unwilling to risk additional German casualties in hand-to-hand combat with the Jews, they had decided to blow up the ghetto, house by house. But the valiant young Jews continued to fight. In some places, such as the bristle factory on Swientojazka Street, the Germans found themselves engaged in fierce battles. Small bands of Jewish fighters flung themselves upon the Germans, killing as many as they could before they themselves were gunned down by the well-armed invaders. Among the heroes of these street battles were the Rodal brothers of Muzonowska Street.

During the days that followed, the Germans sent airplanes to shower the ghetto with phosphorus bombs and other explosives. Within minutes, wide areas of the ghetto were in flames. Walls came crashing down. Roofs collapsed, burying dozens of Jews beneath them. Women and children, trapped in the burning houses, jumped from windows.

On Saturday morning, the third intermediate day of Passover, the buildings on either side of Kupiecka 7 caught fire. When the flames began to lick at our attic, panic broke out. Some, terrified at the thought of being suffocated by the smoke or trapped by the fast-spreading fire, wanted to leave. But Rabbi Zemba ordered them not to go. "Try to put out the flames!" he commanded, and took the lead himself, carrying buckets of water. The people listened to the rabbi and did not leave the hideout.

But by noon the attic was filled with smoke and the flames had reached the steps leading to the attic. Now, at last, Rabbi Zemba led us out of our shelter. But where could we go? We knew that in the streets outside the SS men were waiting to kill the Jews as they emerged from their burning homes. We went down into the basement of the house but we knew that we would not be able to stay there long. We therefore decided, during the next brief lull in the firing, to make for the building across the street, where Reb Beer, the rabbi of Wolle, had been hiding out.

When the firing seemed to have abated for a few moments, Rabbi Zemba's daughter, *Rebbitzin* Rosa Weidenfeld,* looked out the basement window. Apparently not aware that there were SS men in front of the house, she told us to follow her out of the basement and into the adjacent building. She led the way. We saw her signaling to us with her hand. Tragically, we mistook her signal to mean that it was safe for us to proceed. And so we went after her, led by Rabbi Zemba, who was holding his five-year-old grandson, Yankele Ber, by the hand. Suddenly, we heard gunfire, followed by wild screams, coming from the ruins of Nalewki 39. For a split-second, we did not realize what was happening. Rabbi Zemba, only a few steps ahead of us, had fallen to the ground. But we were not able to stop; the steady gunfire drove us back into the basement we had left only moments before.

Until the late afternoon we did not know what had happened to Rabbi Zemba. We hoped against hope that he had merely tripped and fallen, and had somehow managed to escape.

After nightfall, we cautiously ventured outside to see whether there was any trace of the rabbi. We did not have to search for long; his lifeless body lay on the pavement in front of the building.

Somehow, the news of the rabbi's death spread from hideout to hideout. Unmindful of the danger, dozens of his friends and admirers crept out of their shelters to pay

* A daughter-in-law of the late Rabbi of Tchebin, she survived the war and is presently living in Israel.

their last respects to their teacher. Several Torah scholars, constituting themselves as an *ad hoc* court of religious law, decided that Rabbi Zemba's remains should be placed into a temporary grave in the courtyard of Kupiecka 7. As soon as conditions permitted, the scholars ruled, he should be reinterred in the Jewish cemetery.

Late that night, by the eerie light of flames veiled in clouds of smoke, we buried Rabbi Menahem Zemba. Among those present at the scene were two of his daughters, one son-in-law, Reb Beer, and his youngest son, Rabbi Aaron Naftali Zemba,* who recited the mourner's *kaddish*.

Thus ended the life of Rabbi Menahem Zemba, who by his own great example taught his disciples how to live — and, if need be, to die — with the dignity befitting proud, upright Jews.

Based on the story by Rabbi Abraham Zemba in Pesach Almanakh *(New York, 1961).*

---

* He, too, was to die in the ghetto.

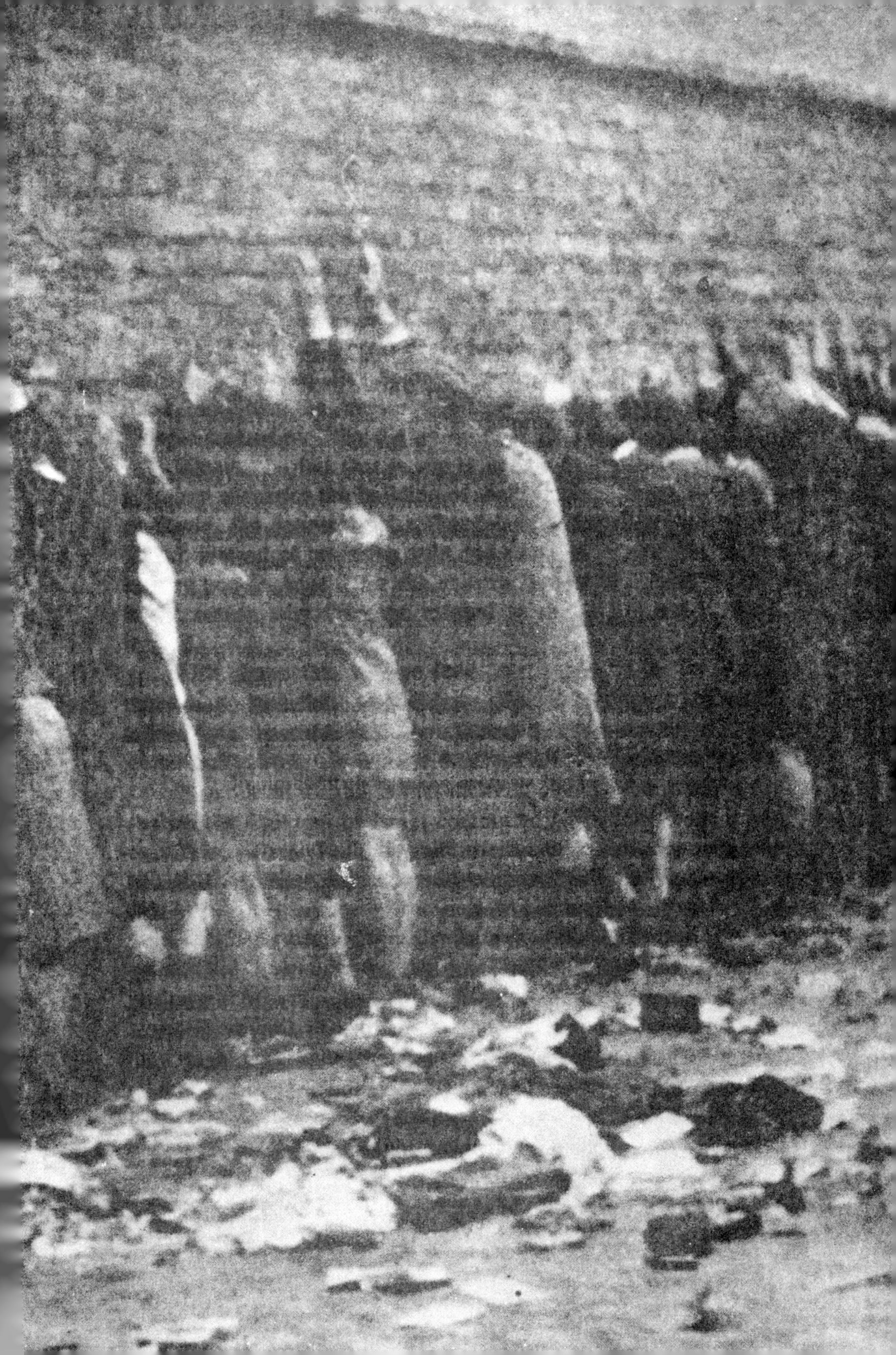

Samson the Mighty

I n the forced labor camp they referred to him simply as "the blacksmith." People in labor camps did not attach importance to such formalities as proper names. But there were some who called this particular blacksmith "Samson the Mighty," for though he was well past middle age, he was a mighty man, not only in physical appearance and bodily strength, but also in qualities of the spirit. He possessed great personal charm which made others want to do as he wished. By nature he was quiet, almost bashful, but when it came to certain questions of personal conduct he knew how to stick by his decisions and no power on earth could sway him, especially in matters of faith and religious observance.

He had been deported from his home town near Vilna in 1944 to the forced labor camp which was run by the German army. The Germans put him to work in the camp's blacksmith shop. There, he soon established a good relationship with the German supervisor, who valued his skills. As a result, the old blacksmith was able to arrive at a private understanding with his German taskmasters: he was to be permitted to observe the Sabbath after a fashion. That is, he would be expected to engage in activities such as handling scrap metal and carrying it from one place to another, which were prohibited only by Rabbinic tradition, but he would be excused from all work that was explicitly forbidden under the Biblical Sabbath law.

Under camp regulations, a roll call was held twice each day: in the morning, before the inmates left the camp for their assigned places of work, and again in the evening, after they had returned to the camp. All the skilled workers would go to their work sites together, in groups. Before leaving the camp, each man was required to "sign out" in a book containing the names of all inmates assigned to "outside work details."

On Saturdays, the blacksmith would leave for work with the rest of his group, but he did not "sign out" because that would have entailed an additional, unwarranted desecration of the Sabbath.

One Saturday morning, shortly before the inmates fell into line to leave for work, Samuel Schneider, the inmate commander, a Jew, sent for the blacksmith and said to him in a voice shaking with terror:

"Why isn't your signature on the outside work list? Did you forget to sign out today? Don't you know what can happen to you if you forget to sign out? Run back and sign out before you get us all into trouble!"

To Schneider's suprise, the blacksmith remained unperturbed. "I didn't *forget* to sign out," he said. "Don't you know it's the Sabbath today and that the Bible forbids us to write on the Sabbath?" That is what the *maggid** had told him in his home town, he declared, and he certainly wasn't the one to ask questions.

Schneider's face was livid with anger and fear.

"Are you out of you mind?" he shouted. "Are you living on the moon? Go and sign you name in the book before they kill us all!"

But the blacksmith was not impressed. He calmly rejoined the others in the line as if Schneider had not been there at all.

When Schneider saw that neither commands nor

---

* Itinerant preacher

threats would help, he called over the work foreman, who was also Jewish, to persuade the blacksmith to sign out, Sabbath or no Sabbath. The foreman came and tried to reason with the stubborn blacksmith. The Germans, he explained, might regard his refusal to sign out as an act of resistance, and heaven alone knew what they would do to him then. But these arguments did not help. The blacksmith stuck to his guns: he would not transgress a law of the Bible, no matter what would befall.

The foreman persisted. He even promised to get the blacksmith a special permit so that he would not have to sign out on future Sabbaths, but couldn't the blacksmith make an exception and sign out just today, on this one Sabbath? After all, wasn't it permissible to violate the Sabbath when human life was endangered? Couldn't he see that his own life, along with the lives of the entire work detail, was at stake?

But then the humble, bashful blacksmith, who had never uttered more than one sentence at a time, opened up and spoke his mind to the foreman. While the other inmates listened in amazement, he spoke of things which no other inmate had ever dared discuss at the camp before: God, faith, and the proper observance of God's commandments even in a Nazi labor camp.

A murmur went through the line of slave laborers. Some whispered in great agitation that the blacksmith's stubbornness would bring disaster upon them all. But there were others who gave him credit for his courage.

The blacksmith ended his oration quietly but with great conviction.

"Gentlemen, I am ready to be killed," he declared, "But you can't make me break the Sabbath."

As it turned out, the fears of Schneider and his foreman did not materialize. Somehow — as though by miracle — the Germans never discovered that one of their slave laborers had failed to sign out on that Saturday morning.

The following Friday, as the blacksmith and his detail prepared to sign out for the day, Schneider quietly called the blacksmith over, turned a page in the book, and told him to sign out in advance for the next morning, so there would be no more arguments about his violating the Sabbath.

That Sabbath morning, as all the inmates stood in line for inspection, the camp commandant, an SS officer, turned up with the work detail book in his hand. Before everyone signed out for the day, he said, he wanted to see whether, by some chance, any one of "his" Jews had signed out in advance the day before. He knew that Jews liked to sleep late on their Sabbath.

The blacksmith stood in his place in line without moving a muscle, but Schneider turned white as chalk. His eyes were riveted to the nervous fingers of the SS man leafing through the book.

But once again a miracle came to pass. Somehow, the camp commandant missed the page on which the blacksmith had signed out one day in advance. The SS man slapped the book shut, turned on his heel and walked away.

For some moments, Schneider stood in utter bewilderment, unable to speak. After he had recovered his composure, he went over to the blacksmith and said to him:

"Now do you understand what you could have done to all of us?"

In answer, the blacksmith gave him a calm and steady look. And so, however briefly, the holiness of the Sabbath eclipsed the evil in the Nazi labor camp.[19]

ᵉᵌ ᵉᵌ ᵉᵌ ᵉᵌ

"Samson the Mighty" was only one of many proud
Jews who were determined to keep alive the traditions of
their fathers even in the death camps. The historian Israel
Gutman, himself not Orthodox (he belonged to the left-
wing HaShomer HaTzair), tells of the respect these up-
holders of the Law inspired in other concentration camp
inmates.

"There was in Auschwitz a group of religious Jews
who would gather clandestinely to pray with a traditional
quorum of ten adult males. Also in Auschwitz, I met a
man who refused to eat non-kosher food and to work on
Sabbaths or holidays. His diet consisted mainly of bread
and water; only on rare occasions did he eat some
vegetables boiled in water. On Saturdays, he would go
with the others to their work site, but he managed for
some time to avoid working on the Sabbath himself. In the
beginning, he was beaten cruelly for refusing to desecrate
the Sabbath, but eventually tasks were found for him that
did not violate the Biblical prohibitions of Sabbath work.
Somehow, this man even succeeded in obtaining a pair of
phylacteries, which he put on every morning. At first we
thought he was insane, but we soon came to respect him
for his strength of conviction and character.[20]

Days of Awe
In Camps And Ghettoes

In the year 1943, as the High Holidays approached, the Tzaddik Reb Yitzhak'l began to worry about how he and his brethren were going to observe the commandment to sound the *shofar* on Rosh HaShanah. There was no *shofar* in the forced labor camp of Skarzysko-Kamienna.

One of Reb Yitzhak'l's followers gave some money to a Gentile inmate and asked him to buy a ram's horn the next time he was assigned to an "outside work detail." Two days later, the Gentile returned with the horn of a cow. Spirits plummeted. Some of the Jewish men tried to convince Reb Yitzhak'l to put the whole thing out of his mind because there would be no way of getting a *shofar* into the labor camp. But Reb Yitzhak'l refused to give up. Once again, he handed some money to the gentile inmate and carefully explained to him that only the horn of a ram would do. This time the Gentile returned with a ram's horn. Now came the task of preparing the crude horn so that it could be sounded properly. Reb Yitzhak'l showed it to Moshe'le Wintertur, who was in the camp's locksmith's workshop, and instructed him to prepare it to the best of his ability. Moshe did not have the slightest idea how to do that, but, to please Reb Yitzhak'l, he took it with him to the workshop. He tinkered with it for quite some time until at last he succeeded in turning the horn into a usable *shofar*. And so, on Rosh HaShanah, 1943, the *shofar* was sounded at Camp Skarzysko-Kamienna.[21]

"On October 5, 1940, the synagogue and house of study of our little town were closed," Shlomo Schmidt, who headed the Jewish community of Fristik during the early part of the Holocaust period, recalled. "And so the Jews planned to hold their holiday services in their homes and in tiny rented rooms in narrow alleys, hoping that the Nazis would not notice.

"By that time most of the able-bodied Jewish men in our town — except, for some reason, the men in the family of the Kolocicer rebbe — had been assigned to labor details by the Nazis. Several days before Yom Kippur, the *Judenrat* — the governing body of our ghetto — bribed two Nazi officials named Hinzeldorf and Radel and in return got permission to supply 100 Jewish workers instead of the usual quota of only 50 on Yom Kippur eve so that the Jews would be able to complete their assigned workload by 12 noon, in time for everyone to prepare for the solemn day, and that no Jew would — Heaven forbid — be forced to work on Yom Kippur. But at ten o'clock on Yom Kippur eve, there arrived a train with ten wagonloads of iron spikes, and the German official in charge of the labor operations announced that the Jews would not be permitted to leave their place of work until all the wagons had been unloaded.

"The rebbe of Kolocice heard the news just as he was about to sit down with his sons for the final meal before the fast. He told his sons to go out at once, join the others at the work site and help unload the wagons so that the Jewish workers would not, heaven forbid, be forced to toil into the evening hours and desecrate the Day of Atonement.

"Unfortunately, the Germans had forgotten all about their promise to the *Judenrat*. They announced that anyone leaving the work site before evening would be shot. The Jews were also forced to report for work on the next day, Yom Kippur itself."[22]

One Yom Kippur eve, the rabbis of the town of Kletzk went from house to house to beg the Jews not to absent themselves from their work the next day, for it was obvious that if they did not report for work as usual, even on Yom Kippur, they would all be killed. Accordingly, the Jews fasted throughout the day but followed their regular work routine in the German army barracks: They were harnessed to wagons like beasts of burden to remove the garbage and manure from the horses' stables.[23]

"The Nazis were driven by a ferocious hatred for the Jewish religion and Jewish religious leaders," B. Stick, a survivor of the Rozwadow concentration camp, recalled.

"On Yom Kippur, 1942, the Jewish inmates of Camp Rozwadow were forced to work, as usual, at the Stalowa-Wola forced labor camp. At the end of Yom Kippur, the German commandant summoned Rabbi Fraenkel, an inmate who had lived in Wieliczka, near Cracow, before the war and said to him: 'I know you did not do any work today, because it was your holiday. So I'm going to kill you.' And he shot him then and there."[24]

Yom Kippur
in Czestochowa — 1942

On the day before Yom Kippur, 1942, the German occupation authorities in Czestochowa sent for R. Henoch Gabriel of Bodzanov, who was living in the city and was known to have a large number of followers there.

When the rabbi, a man of 70, arrived at the German headquarters, he was instructed to have all his ablebodied followers report the next day for forced labor.

The rabbi replied that he would not send other Jews out to work on Yom Kippur. "If you want Jews to work for you tomorrow, " he told the Germans, "you will have to find them yourselves, and take them by force."

The Nazis retorted that if he would not send them any Jews for work the next day, he would be shot.

"Very well, then," the rabbi said to the German officer. "If that's the case, I am ready to die."

No Jews reported for work on Yom Kippur in Czestochowa. On the day after Yom Kippur, the Germans dragged the aged rabbi from his home and shot him.

Based on a letter reprinted in The Jewish Daily Forward,
April 12, 1945.

A Rosh HaShanah Sermon

I always pray with the Gerer Hasidim during the High Holidays. Every year I come away from them strengthened and revived. For me, praying at the Gerer *shtibel* on New York's West Side is an act of spiritual regeneration. It is not only the *davening;* it is also the tales which the Hasidim exchange in between their prayers.

Last year, for instance, on the second day of Rosh HaShanah, a Gerer Hasid told me a story which sounded like a prayer in its own right. Perhaps future generations will read it each year before they recite the *Unetane Tokef,* the awe-inspiring narrative of the martyrdom of Rabbi Amnon of Mayence that has been told and retold for so many centuries. It almost seemed as if fate had brought me to the Gerer *shtibel* in New York so that I might hear this story and pass it on.

It happened in the fall of 1944, during the final year of the war, at Siegmar-Schoenau, a concentration camp in Lower Saxony. The last transport of survivors from the ghetto of Lodz had just arrived from Auschwitz, which the Germans were slowly evacuating as the advancing Russian armies drew closer. There were only a few days left until Rosh HaShanah. Starved Jews, their bloated bodies wrapped in rags, were preparing for the Days of Awe. A group of young men at the camp spread the word that they would organize religious services for their fellow inmates. Religious services in the nethermost depths of hell, under the very eyes of the Nazi murderers? It seemed foolhardy, almost insane. And yet, perhaps for this very reason, the plan was received with enthusiasm and one of the barracks was chosen to serve as a synagogue.

On the first evening of Rosh HaShanah, after roll call, several hundred Jews made their way to the designated barrack. Among them were old men and young boys, traditionalists and freethinkers, and even a sprinkling of Jewish kapos* and "privileged characters" whom we despised as stooges for the Germans.

Because there were no prayer books, it was decided that the role of cantor should be assigned to someone with a background of Jewish learning who would be able to recite all the prayers by heart. The congregation would repeat the prayers after him, verse for verse.

Among those who attended that service and survived the war** was the man who told me this story at the Gerer shtibel and who, in fact, is the hero of the tale. His name is Simon Zuker, and he hails from Lodz.

Prayers in the barrack at Siegmar-Schoenau had begun quietly and solemnly, but before long, the calm, measured words were drowned in bitter sobs. Each person remembered his home, his loved ones, and the holidays of years gone by, when Europe still had thousands of synagogues, large and small, with millions of men, women and children to pray in them. Those who had gathered for prayer behind the barbed wire fences of the Nazi concentration camp were mourning the dead and the living alike; they wept for worlds that had vanished, and for

* Camp trusties.

** Among the others were Yosef Mayer Seidel, now a shohet in Mexico; Pinchas Rosenfeld and his two sons, and Solek Weltfried, all of whom have settled in Israel; David Klein, Leibel Lewkowitz, Shmuel Gliksman and Abraham Dziadek, who are now in New York, and Ephraim England, who has made his home in Denver.

houses of prayer and study that had gone up in flames. The tears flowed like rivers, never to cease, it seemed, until the Master of the Universe would take pity on His people at long last and decree an end to their sufferings.

After the *Shemone Esreh*, just before the *Alenu* prayer, which speaks of the day when God will be recognized as King over all the earth, the inmate Simon Zuker stepped forward and delivered a sermon. Why was he not afraid? If the Germans had ever found out — and there was no lack of informers at Siegmar-Schoenau — that he had "made a speech" to his fellow inmates, his life would not have been worth a penny. But now, in New York, twenty years later, Zuker told me what had impelled him to deliver his sermon that night. It seems that suddenly he had seen before his eyes, with the utmost clarity, the face of the aged Gerer *rebbe*, and then himself as a young man, in the midst of thousands of other Hasidim who had left their homes and families each year to spend Rosh HaShanah with the *rebbe*. This shining vision of a long-lost world had given Simon Zuker the strength to rise and address his fellow inmates at the concentration camp.

"My brothers," he said, "this is the first night of Rosh HaShanah. We are crushed, bruised, starved, and we are mourning our lost homes and families. But, as I have just said, it is Rosh HaShanah and it is our duty to try to do as we did in our home towns every year. In those days, after prayers, we would go to our parents, to our wives and children, and to our friends to wish them a good new year. But today — who knows where they all are now? Let us do it in spirit, then. Let us think of our loved ones, send our words heavenward and hope that our thoughts may reach them — sometime, somewhere."

As Zuker spoke, the weeping in the crowded barrack grew louder. But he continued:

"Let us remember also that this is a holiday. Soon it

will be time to recite the festival *kiddush*. But we have neither wine nor *hallah*. Not even a crust of dry bread has remained from today's rations. Still, we must recite the *kiddush*. Let us, therefore, fill our tin cups with our tears, and, with our tears for wine, sanctify Rosh HaShanah before the Master of the Universe ... "

Years later, Simon Zuker was to say that his speech had been inspired by a courage born of desperation. But his Rosh HaShanah sermon had not been the counsel of despair. He reminded his fellow inmates that they had moral obligations to fulfill even in concentration camp. He urged them to continue observing the precepts of loving kindness, to help the sick, hold up the fallen and comfort those smarting and bruised from Nazi floggings.

Simon Zuker did not then expect to live until the end of the nightmare, but he survived, and he has rebuilt his life in America. Now, twenty years after his Rosh HaShanah sermon, he stood beside me in the Gerer *shtibel* in New York, rapt in his prayers. And I felt that as he poured out his heart to God here, in the land of freedom, he saw before his closed eyes not only the Gerer *rebbe* and the Hasidim of long ago, but the entire congregation which had wept and prayed together with him at Siegmar-Schoenau on that last Rosh HaShanah of the war. And as I relived that night with him in my own thoughts, I wondered when a new Reb Levi Isaac of Berditchev would arise and cry out: "Master of the Universe, I defy Thee to name me one other people who, in the midst of such cruelty and despair, would have gathered together to praise Thee as the Sovereign of the Universe!"

Translated and adapted by Gertrude Hirschler from Elie Wiesel's article in The Daily Forward, *August 5, 1965.*

4.

Study As a Way of Survival

THE UNCONQUERABLE SPIRIT

Study as a Life Preserver

Before the war, Torah study had been a way of life for hundreds of thousands of Jews in Eastern Europe. During the Holocaust years, it was to serve many of them as a way of survival. Skeptics have labeled this constant preoccupation with Talmudic studies as an attempt to escape from the harsh realities of life in the ghettoes and concentration camps. But they cannot deny that the unceasing study of Torah enabled countless Jews in the camps and ghettoes to go on living worthily until the end, and in some cases even to survive physically and spiritually until the day of liberation.

In the French resort town of Vitel the Germans had set up an internment camp for citizens of countries not under Nazi occupation. Among the internees were Jews who, with the help of friends or relatives in Switzerland, had obtained citizenship papers of Latin American republics and were therefore immune to deportation. But they lived in a state of constant fear and uncertainty. How long would their reprieve last? Would the Germans change their minds and deport them after all? And what of the relatives and friends who had not been fortunate enough to obtain the coveted foreign documents? Some already knew that their loved ones had been taken from their homes to unknown destinations. There was nothing to do now but to live from day to day as best one could, to keep one's sanity.

There were several Orthodox families in Vitel, among them the Rapoports, the Weingurts and the Fraenkels, all from the Polish town of Bielice. Rabbi Joseph Fraenkel, one of his sons, Alexander, had married a daughter of R. Meir Alter, the Gerer *rebbe*, was in regular correspondence with another son, Shabse Fraenkel, who was then living in Brooklyn. The father's letters said little about the problems of life in an internment camp. The father did not beg his son in America to rescue him. He merely impressed upon him, over and over again, the importance of setting aside a period each day for the study of Torah. At Camp Vitel, the Orthodox men spent most of their days in the study of the Law and in strengthening religious morale among their fellow internees. They assembled prayer quorums for daily worship and somehow even managed to construct a ritual bath in the cellar of the hotel where they were quartered. And one day Camp Vitel was the scene of a real celebration: a group of men had completed the study of the entire Mishnah and marked the occasion with a festive gathering, complete with a good meal and learned discourses, as they might have done in their home towns before the days of war and persecution.

Eventually, alas, the Germans liquidated Camp Vitel. Among those who had not found a way to emigrate was Rabbi Joseph Fraenkel. Along with the other remaining internees, he was deported to a German concentration camp at Drancy, near Paris. From there, he was sent to Auschwitz. He did not survive the war.[25]

Jews who had been far from religious before the war turned to the Torah for spiritual sustenance in the camps and the ghettoes. Jacob Rasson, a survivor of a Latvian concentration camp, has told the story of a young man from Riga who found his way back to Judaism at Camp Poprovalna:

"His name was Levin, and he hailed from Riga. A

fair-haired young man of about 30, he held university degrees in law and biology, was an expert in German literature and a scholar also in other European languages. He was a man of broad education and culture. All his life he had considered himself a freethinker and had given little thought to his Jewish heritage. His first encounter with Orthodox Jews was in the Riga ghetto. The unwavering faith of these people, expressed in their painstaking observance of law and ritual even in virtual imprisonment, had a profound impact on Levin, and he joined them in their sessions of Torah study.

"By the time I first met him in Camp Poprovalna, he was already a deeply religious Jew, firmly rooted in the foundations of Jewish tradition. He enjoyed discussing the religious and national aspects of Judaism and at times succeeded in convincing other skeptics, as he himself once had been, that no matter how hopeless the present might appear, God was still the Sovereign of the universe, and that the only way to live a life of human dignity even at the concentration camp was to be strict in the observance of God's Law.

"Levin was careful to recite his prayers three times each day. Twice a week — on Mondays and Thursdays — he did not eat his meager rations but gave them to other inmates, especially the sick and the weak.

"As a rule, he would recite the daily evening service with friends who had become his disciples. Afterwards, he would deliver a lecture on a religious theme. And as we stood before him, crowded into the dark barracks, we forgot, for one brief hour, the torments, the beatings, the shootings and the hangings that were our lot at Camp Poprovalna."[26]

Abraham Hendeles, one of the survivors of the Jewish community of Warsaw, recalls:

"Shortly before Passover, 1941, I sent my younger

brother Jonathan — who was later killed by the Nazis — to deliver matzoth to all the rabbis and Hasidic *rebbes* in the ghetto. When he returned to my hideout, Jonathan reported to me that wherever he went, he had come upon groups of Jews who were spending their days at study and prayer. It was known that clandestine prayer meetings were held at various private homes. I myself visited several such 'underground' *shtiblech*, where Jews met to worship and study at the risk of their lives.

"One such place was the apartment of R. Abraham Hayyim Danziger, brother of the *rebbe* of Aleksandrow. (The *rebbe*, R. Isaac Menahem Danziger, later died in Treblinka). R. Abraham's apartment was on the fourth floor of Milewska 3. Regular services were held also at Milewska 5, at the homes of R. David Gelbart, a Hassid of Sochaczew, and Yankel Bash, a Mezhirich Hassid."[27]

Even the non-religious admired their pious brethren for their strength of conviction. In 1961 Dr. Herman Kruk, a self-declared atheist, published the diary he kept while in the Vilna ghetto. In the entry dated April 24, 1942, he makes mention of the activities of the Orthodox during that period:

"I want to add that the Orthodox in the ghetto were not idle. There are two yeshivot — one, an academy for higher Talmudic studies, the other, a day school for young boys."[28]

The Nazis and the Scholars

Very early in the war, the Nazis realized that Torah study, and the scholars who taught the Torah, played a crucial role in the spiritual survival of their Jewish victims. No wonder that they developed an almost fanatical hatred for scholars and students of the Law.

The following is the entry for November 4, 1943 by Eliezer Yerushalmi, who kept a diary of his experiences in the ghetto of Siauliai, Lithuania.

"Hauptsturmfuhrer Foerster arrived from Kovno, and immediately went off to see his shoemaker [one of the inmates]. At the cobbler's workshop, he came across a Jewish inmate who was busy studying the Gemarah. Foerster slapped his face and shouted: 'You don't have to study your holy writings now![29] Don't you know there's a war on?' "

During 1941 many rabbis, scholars and religious functionaries in Lithuania were killed. Aware of the Nazi hatred for Jewish religious leaders, many rabbis removed their beards, exchanged their Hasidic garb for ordinary clothing and lived in the ghettoes as ordinary manual workers.[30]

The Nazis regarded rabbis and Hasidic *rebbes* as potential ringleaders of ghetto revolts. Thus, in the ghetto of Lodz, rabbis, particularly members of the ghetto's rabbinical council, were among the first to be arrested and murdered. Rabbi Shmuel David Laski, Rabbi Mendel Rosenmutter, Rabbi Abraham Silman (who had married into the dynasty of Ger) and Rabbi Fishel Rabbinowitz managed to go underground and hide out for some time, but were eventually caught and deported. The identity of the man responsible for the murder of Rabbi Rabbinowitz is known: he was a Gestapo officer by the name of Guenther Fuchs.

Another Holocaust survivor, Elimelekh HaKohen Schwartz, recalls that during the period of the so-called "curfews," forty rabbis were deported from the Lodz ghetto. These rabbis had come to the city from small villages nearby, hoping to be safe among their brethren in the large ghetto community. Among those deported was Schwartz's own brother-in-law, R. Yerachmiel Wilbromsky, a young scholar from the Polish town of Lutomiersk.

In an attempt to elude death, illustrious rabbinic scholars toiled in the Lodz ghetto as simple laborers. After working all day at the most menial tasks imaginable, they would spend the evening hours teaching Torah and strengthening the morale of the other ghetto inmates.

On the second day of Rosh HaShanah, 1942, the Germans conducted a full scale search for rabbis and Hasidic *rebbes* in the ghetto of Lodz. The rabbis were taken to the headquarters of the *Judenrat* — the governing body of the ghetto — and from there to the death camps.[31]

A Yeshiva Goes Into Hiding

The Jewish community of Dembitz, a small town in Galicia, had never been large or wealthy, but it had always taken an active interest in Torah study.

Several years before World War II, R. Israel Leib Fraenkel, a young Belzer Hasid of about 30, had founded a yeshiva in Dembitz. Following the Nazi conquest, the original student body of the yeshiva dispersed, but before long, R. Israel Leib had gathered around him a new

nucleus of boys between the ages of 14 and 16. Classes were held in the attic of a man named Joseph Rosch. Under the circumstances, the survival of the yeshiva was truly a miracle.

Classes began every morning at 8:30 with a lesson in Gemarah — Tractate Sabbath — with the various classic commentaries. In the afternoon, the students reviewed the morning's lesson. The evening hours were devoted to secular studies.

R. Leib did not restrict his lessons to straightforward Talmudic law. He always introduced elements of mysticism into his lectures to keep up the morale of his students. When the boys were dismayed by reports of German victories on the Russian front, R. Israel explained that these early successes were, in fact, portents of defeat for Germany and of deliverance for the Jews. His

courage and optimism remained with him until the end. Along with 200 other Jews from Dembitz, R. Israel was deported to the slave labor camp of Postkow, where he met his death.

Another Torah scholar active in Dembitz during the early part of the war was R. Moshe Schmidt, who had come there as a refugee from Cracow late in 1940. He had been known as an outstanding teacher and had served as examiner of candidates for admission to the famous Yeshiva of Lublin. In Dembitz, R. Moshe began to give lessons in Talmudic debate, an activity he continued until the winter of 1941, when he was deported to the concentration camp of Radomsko. When the Germans informed him in the summer of 1942 that he was going to be sent back to Dembitz, he marched out onto the main highway with his Torah scroll in his arms and declared that he would not return to the town from which he had been deported. He would not go back to a place where, in all likelihood, there were no Jews left, he said. The Nazis shot him at once.[32]

Even at Postkow, the slave labor camp to which R. Israel Leib Fraenkel was deported, there were inmates who never stopped studying the Torah. After the war, survivors told the story of R. Elimelech Steier, who had worked as a Torah journalist before the war. Even under the most difficult conditions imaginable, R. Elimelech put on his *tefillin* every morning and refused to eat non-kosher food. Whatever free time he had he spent conducting informal Bible classes for his fellow inmates, lecturing from memory since he had no books with him. His favorite book was the Book of Proverbs. When he was asked the reason for his preference, he replied: "The Hebrew consonants in *Mishle* (Proverbs) are *mem, shin, lamed* and *yud*. These consonants also form the initials for the work I am trying to do here: 'Melech *Sh*teier Lernt Yiddishkeit' — Melech Shteier is teaching Judaism."[33]

Study As A Weapon

During the Holocaust, as 'for centuries before, many Orthodox Jews believed that the evil in this world could not be defeated by physical warfare, because the struggle between good and evil would eventually be decided not by human force but by Divine Providence. Thus, while some rabbis and scholars of the Law in the ghettoes of Eastern Europe approved of armed resistance and even participated personally in underground work, others were convinced that self-refinement through prayer and study was the only weapon which Jews could wield against the archenemy.

In this spirit, Jews of all ages and walks of life sat together in ghetto basements and attics, immersing themselves in the study of the Law. Examples of unswerving devotion to Torah study in the face of overwhelming odds and ever-present danger abounded not only in the ghettoes of larger Jewish communities such as Warsaw, Lodz, or Vilna, but also in much smaller towns and villages where Jews lived in scattered handfuls.

In Makow-Mazowiecki, where, according to an eyewitness report, "the situation in the ghetto was such that no one could be sure whether he would not be dead a few moments hence", twenty boys hid out in a tiny, dark attic and devoted all their waking hours to the study of the Law. In Demblin Modzitz, Moshe Lichtenstein, one of the leaders of the Jewish community, a man of about 50, sat day and night over his holy books.

In Kotzk, as a survivor reports, "men — old men in

particular — sat and studied the Torah, which they searched for allegories and numerological hints to show that the end of Hitler and his cohorts was at hand. They sought to hasten deliverance by tears, by study and by prayer."

In Ostrowiec, Reb Mordechai, head of the renowned Yeshiva in which that community had justly taken pride before the war, moved into a tiny, sloping attic with his family and a few of the students who were still alive. "There, in two narrow cells, they barricaded themselves against the foe; there, they were able to sit undisturbed over Torah and good works; there, they were able to serve the Lord."

The Bunker Of The Hasidim

The following account is taken from the diary kept by Dr. Hillel Seidman, author and journalist, during the years he spent in the Warsaw ghetto. Dr. Seidman, who was active in Orthodox Jewish communal life in Poland, is now living in the United States.

Today I had an unusual experience: I paid a visit to an underground world. This morning two young men, Manes Rosenstrauch and the son of the Agudath Israel leader Benjamin W. Hendeles, came to me with a summons: "We're going to have a meeting at No. 35 Nalewki Street at five o'clock this afternoon. You will be there also." What kind of meeting it was, and who had called it, they did not say, nor did I ask them. You don't ask questions in the ghetto. When you are told that you are expected to appear at a certain place at a given time, it is clear that you must be there without fail, for such an invitation is equivalent to a command. We have become accustomed to the discipline of the ghetto.

And so, five minutes before five o'clock this afternoon, I passed through the gate of 35 Nalewki Street. A boy in a Hasidic-style hat (the Hasidic boys are the only ones who still insist on traditional Jewish dress; all the others, even the most Orthodox, have taken to wearing ordinary caps) was already there, waiting for me. When he saw me, he simply said, "Come."

He led the way, and I followed. I knew the house

well. It belonged to our friend, Jacob Trockenheim, a wealthy man who had been a member of the Polish Senate before the war.* But now the building seemed to have been transformed into an unending network of secret passages. We passed through one courtyard, then a second, and a third. From there, we descended into a cellar about two stories beneath the surface of the street. We kept on walking, until we emerged into another building, 11 Kupiecka Street. My young escort led me up several flights of steps. On the top floor of 11 Kupiecka was a small room in which there stood a ladder; it led to the attic of the building. After reaching the attic, we walked through a narrow, dark corridor. Now we had come into a third building — 38 Zamenhof Street. Here, the shutters were closed, forcing us to grope our way through complete darkness down a few more flights of steps. At last, we arrived in the basement. The room through which we now passed was furnished with some crude benches and several wooden reading stands. There were books all over. It was a *bet midrash*, a study room like so many others throughout Warsaw's Jewish neighborhoods, where men of all ages pored over sacred texts. But we had not yet reached our destination. My guide led me into an adjoining room. That room was bare, except for what looked like a furnace at one end. The young man opened the furnace door and walked straight in, leaving me rooted to the spot in confusion. Seeing my bewilderment, he turned around and called to me, "Come." I crawled through the furnace door after him, and found myself in a low, narrow tunnel. The tunnel led into another room where there was a trapdoor. I followed my escort down a rope ladder which seemed to have no end. At long last, I felt hard ground beneath my feet again. I looked around. I was now in a clean, spacious room lit by an electric lamp. The walls of

* Trockenheim, a leader in the Agudath Israel movement, represented the Orthodox Jews in the Polish Parliament. He did not survive the war.

the room were lined with long benches; in the middle of the room was a long table of unpolished wood around which stood some young men, obviously yeshiva students.

The students led me through a door into another room, this one small and dark. There, they showed me an electric oven, a gas range, and a supply closet filled with groceries.

"How long could this food supply hold out?" I asked my escort. "It depends on the number of people who'd be taking shelter here," he replied. "We figure we have enough to feed 120 people for eight months."

"By that time, things should be settled one way or the other," one of the young students chimed in.

This, then, was the bunker of the Hasidim. It was set up by three capable young men — Klepfish, Oppenheim, Seidenbeutel — all engineers. It is situated beneath a bombed-out building of which little has remained on the surface except a pile of rubble. What is left of the gate and the walls has been fenced in with barbed wire. No one would think that human beings could be living in relative comfort beneath this mess.

The bunker of the Hasidim is, in fact, a complete apartment with all the amenities of a home — electric light, water, gas and toilet facilities. The food supply closet is amply stocked with flour, vegetables, ersatz honey, zwieback and canned goods.

I could only marvel at the resourcefulness of the men who set up this bunker. After the war, I will gather as many Polish engineers as I will be able to find and take them on an inspection tour of the premises. I will show them what Jewish brains were able to devise under conditions that defied the imagination.

After duly admiring the arrangements, I became

acquainted with some of the older people who had already taken up residence in the bunker. First of all, there was the well-known cantor, Gershon Sirota.* He had been brought to the bunker by his son, the chairman of the Jewish Relief Society. Then there was Feibish, former president of the Jewish community of Lodz, and Shimon Folman, a musician who had served as conductor of the ghetto's symphony orchestra. It occurred to me that there was, here in the bunker, an array of talent sufficient to put together a concert. Indeed, there was music in the bunker, but it was not the kind of music one might expect to hear in a concert hall. It was the chant of Talmudic study, coming from another room. I listened in amazement.

Without a word, my escort led me into the room from where the singsong came. What I saw there reminded me of the tales of the Tannaites who had studied the Torah in caves, hiding from the Roman oppressors, and the historical accounts of the Marranos who observed their Jewish faith in secret chambers, away from the prying eyes of the Spanish Inquisition. But the scene I now beheld was not of the past: it was the reality of our own present day. Around a long table, heads bent over open folios, sat about 20 yeshiva students, "learning" Gemarah with devout enthusiasm. They were discussing the laws of "forbidden mixtures." Their diligent study is their way of hurling their defiance at the enemy outside, their proclamation that, no matter what may befall, they will never abandon the Law and the God of their fathers.

The faces of the boys were pale, and their eyes shone with an other-worldly fire. Most of them have already lost their families. The *rebbes* who taught them before the war and from whom they might have drawn

* Sirota (1874-1943) was one of the first cantors to have his voice recorded. At one time he toured the United States but refused offers of positions there and returned to Poland. He and his family perished in the Warsaw ghetto.

solace are also gone. But they have been adopted by a new *rebbe*, Rabbi Judah Leib Landa of Kolobiel. Before the war, Rabbi Landa headed the famous Yeshiva of Lublin.* Now he comes to the boys in this bunker twice each week to lecture to them on the sacrifices offered in the Temple. Unfortunately he was not there this afternoon; he was delivering a learned discourse to 30 other students in a room on Mila Street.

I already knew some of the boys who were seated around that long table in the bunker. In addition to Hendeles and Manes Rosenstrauch, who had "invited" me to join them, there were Elbinger, grandson of the rabbi of Lublin, Rabbi Shlomo Eger; Nathan Beharia, grandson of the rebbe of Sochatchov; Aaron Zemba, son of Rabbi Menachem Zemba;** and Leibel Alter, grandson of the Gerer rebbe. There also were several older men, David Elimelech Kupfer and Abraham Zaken Feldwebel, who were active as educators in the Agudath Israel before the war.***

The men who set up the bunker regard this miniature yeshiva as their second home. They have put a lot of time and money into the project. At first, the tenants in adjacent buildings, who are not Orthodox, had little use for the "fanatical" young men who were unwilling to give up their "Jewish hats" and long sidecurls. Later, however, they came to view these "exotic types" with curiosity and interest, and now they even look upon them with some respect.

The "meeting" to which I had been invited had

* The building which housed that yeshiva in Warsaw before the war is now used by a medical school.

** For an account of Rabbi Zemba's last days, see "The Last Seder of R. Menachem Zemba", pp. 75-86.

*** Feldwebel had been director of the teacher's seminary of Agudath Israel in Warsaw. Neither he nor Kupfer survived the war.

begun. A tall, thin lad with ascetic features acted as chairman.

"Joseph (Szcaranski) who used to work for the Lublin Yeshiva before the war, has informed me that there is a way in which we could 'legalize' our status here in the ghetto," he reported. "We could obtain identity papers and get jobs at Herman Bauer's workshop on 38 Nalewki Street. Then we'd stop being outcasts (that is, Jews living in the ghetto without official identification papers). Also, we would be entitled to ration cards for bread and soup. Oh, yes, there would be a kosher kitchen for us at the workshop. The purpose of this meeting is to take a vote on whether we should stay as we are, or whether we should 'go legal.' "

"And how does this group feel about 'going legal'?" I asked.

For a few moments, no one spoke. Finally, young Elbinger, a boy of 18, got up and requested the floor.

"As far as I'm concerned," he said, "I've made my decision. I'm not going to 'go legal,' I'll stay right here in the bunker. But then, of course, I can't speak for the others in this room. You will have to give the matter some more thought."

"And why don't you want to 'go legal'?" I asked him.

"Very simple," Elbinger replied. "The Germans are our enemies, regardless of whether we have official papers or not. What advantages would there be in 'going legal'? How many people whom we know have registered with the authorities these three years that we've been in this ghetto? I think no more than ten. I never registered. If we register, we'll be called to work wherever the Germans decide we should go. How do we know to what place they'll send us? How do we know whether we'll be able to keep from working on the Sabbath, and whether we'll have kosher food? Register with the authorities? Not me! Sure, the Germans are forever threatening to kill any Jew who fails to register and obtain proper identity papers. So what? Why should they get to me, of all people? 'Legal' or not, there's always the chance that we'll end up being deported. But at least as long as I'm not registered, I won't find my name on the official list of those 'invited' to proceed to the railroad station for a trip to a concentration camp. If we stay here and forget about 'going legal', we may have a better chance to escape being deported and to hold out until it's all over."

After some more discussion, I volunteered to investigate both aspects of the question: first, the problem of whether or not we should even consider "going legal;" and second, how we would be able to get kosher food. I undertook to ask the advice of such communal leaders as Rabbi Menachem Zemba, Rabbi David Shapiro,* Rabbi Zvi Ari Frommer (head of the Yeshiva of Kuziglov), Rabbi Alexander Z. Friedman,** Abraham Gepner [who was a wealthy industrialist before the war], Isaac Giterman [who headed the Warsaw office of the American Jewish Joint Distribution Committee before the United States had entered the war], and David Guzik.***

---

* Rabbi Shapiro survived the war and eventually settled in West Germany, serving as rabbi in the city of Fuerth until his death.

** Rabbi Friedman was one of the leaders of organized Orthodox Polish Jewry between the two world wars. Though he was widely active as a speaker, writer and religious administrator, his basic interest was in educational work and Rabbinic scholarship. He was deported to the death camp of Travniki, Lublin district, and killed by the Germans in November, 1943.

*** David Guzik survived the war and helped the American Jewish Joint Distribution Committee in its postwar relief work. He was killed in an airplane crash.

The Underground Yeshiva

Mrs. Bella Scharfherz, a survivor of the Warsaw ghetto, vividly recalls the intensity and devotion with which the Hasidim in the Warsaw ghetto carried on their Torah studies.

"During the ghetto period our house on Novolipje Street 39 was turned into a sort of Hasidic center! Couriers from all the groups and *shtiblech* of Gerer Hasidim in the Warsaw ghetto went in and out of that house. They came with requests for all kinds of help, particularly food. We used to receive food packages from relatives in the Radomsk ghetto and David (David Neistadter, my late first husband) would distribute the groceries to the students who were hiding out in attics and basements studying the Torah ...

"From among the couriers who came to our house for food I particularly remember Rabbi Hershel Rappaport, who was the spiritual advisor of the Hasidim in the ghetto,* and one daring young man whom everybody called 'Prager.' These two men had taken on the task of collecting food for the Hasidim who had gone into hiding.

"On one occasion I visited the famous 'Hasidic Bunker,' because David spent a lot of time there. From time to time, he would leave our house and move into the bunker to study with the Hasidim. The young Hasidim

---

* Before the war, Rabbi Rappaport had been a professor at the teachers' seminary of Agudath Israel in Warsaw.

used to call him 'Commandant!,* David had no fear whatsoever that the Germans might discover him, and he had
no intention of giving up any of our religious observances.

"David gave me secret instructions how to reach the
bunker. You had to enter the courtyard on Kupiecka
Street; from there you got to a house on Nalewki Street —
first to the attic and then down many steps to the cellar. I
had to knock on the wall twice — this was a prearranged
signal — and say that I was David's wife. This was the
only way I could gain admittance to the hideout.

"I'll never forget that bunker. The cellar was divided
into several small rooms. The whole place was lit by carbide lamps. There were Gemarah volumes and other holy
books all over the place. The men sat there, studying with
great enthusiasm. I saw a number of yeshiva students
whom I knew. There was Yossel Rosenblum of Lodz, and
another Lodz boy, the son of Moshe Cederbaum.* There
was also a young Hasid who was lame; his name was
Bernstein. Altogether, there must have been about 20 men
in that bunker — perhaps a little more. There was a small
oven and I noticed some cooking utensils.

"All this happened over 30 years ago, but it's still
hard for me to talk about those days. If you ask me, those
boys who studied in that bunker were as brave and daring
as any of the ghetto fighters."

* Youth groups of Gerer Hasidim would refer to their group leaders as
"Commandant."

* Moshe Cederbaum, a wealthy textile manufacturer before the war,
had been known as the "king of the textile industry" in Poland. At one
time he employed 3,000 workers.

5.

At the End

A Sage is Better than a Prophet

The Perfect Memorial

THE UNCONQUERABLE SPIRIT

A Sage Is Better Than A Prophet

I was aboard one of the transports of Jews from Auschwitz traveling west into the heartland of Germany. It was late in April, 1945, and the Germans, beaten on every front, were evacuating the death camps in the East to flee from the advancing Soviet forces. We knew that the war was almost over, but we wondered whether we would be able to hold out until the hour of liberation.

Among the Jews in our car was Rabbi Yekutiel Judah Halberstam, the *rebbe* of Klausenburg. A man barely 40 years old, he had lost his wife and 11 children in the Holocaust. Yet he was able to speak words of consolation to us. Freedom, he said, was at hand. Hold out until then, and all will yet be well.

On the fourth day of our journey a German officer entered our car and shouted: "Germany has surrendered! You're all free now!" Hearing this, the prisoners stampeded to the doors of the car and began to jump off the train. But the *rebbe* remained in his place. He feared that the announcement was a German trap and he wanted to hold us back. "Before we leave this train," he shouted, "let us recite the *Hallel* to give thanks to God for our liberation!" And so we began to pray. As we recited the psalms of thanksgiving, we could hear the crack of gunfire outside.

Afterwards, we learned that the *rebbe* of Klausenburg had been right. The report of the German surrender had been a ruse aimed to get the Jews off the train, the easier to be able to shoot them. Those of our comrades — alas, 400 of them — who had left the train were killed almost as soon as they hit the ground.

Those of us who had remained in the car to pray had been saved from certain death by the *rebbe's* wisdom.

After the war, the *rebbe* settled in Brooklyn, where he re-established the dynasty of Klausenburg. In 1956, he moved to Natanya, Israel where he set up Kiryat Tzans, a stronghold of Hasidism rooted in the old-new Homeland of the Jewish people.

Based on Michael Bar-On, *Sefer Szamosvar*, p. 88.

The Perfect Memorial

A mong the Torah scrolls in the synagogue of Brooklyn's Yeshiva Torah Vodaath there is one dedicated to the everlasting memory of "Aryeh ben Leah Kornblit and his wife," who perished in the Holocaust.

Memorials such as these are, alas, not rare. Many of those who were spared in the slaughter of European Jewry have had Torah scrolls written to perpetuate the names of loved ones whose final resting place is unknown. But this Torah scroll in the yeshiva synagogue is unique in that the initial payment for it was made not by the survivors, but by the two martyrs whose names are embroidered on its velvet mantle.

The story of how this came to be was told by Rabbi Israel Shapiro, the venerable *rebbe* of the Polish town of Bluszow, who is now living in Brooklyn. Rabbi Shapiro himself is a survivor of the death camp of Yanowka, near Lwow, from which only 11 out of 3,000 inmates emerged alive at the time of liberation.

Late in the evening of January 13, 1943 a *kapo* had entered the barracks where the *rebbi* slept, and called for the "*rebbe* of Bluszow" to get up. The *rebbi* did not move, and no one else in the barrack stirred. No one thought anything else but that the *rebbi* was about to be singled out for special torture. However, when the *kapo*, himself a Jew, reassured the inmates that nothing would happen to the *rebbe*, but that he had an important message for him, Rabbi Shapiro himself arose from his bunk and came forward.

"I am Rabbi Shapiro," he said.

The *kapo* put into his hand a crumpled envelope. The *rebbe* opened the envelope and drew out a sheet of paper, on which there was the following note, scribbled in pencil. Whoever had written the note had clearly had not much time to spare.

January 13, 1943

My dear Rabbi Israel Shapiro, may you have a long and happy life!

They have just surrounded the bristle factory in the ghetto where some 800 of us have been working, and we are about to be put to death. The only question they are still debating is whether they should shoot us on the spot or take us to the ovens.

Please, dear Rabbi, if you should be found worthy of

being saved, and if you should be able to settle in the Land of Israel, see to it that, somewhere upon our holy soil, a little marker is put up with my wife's name and my own so that our names should not be forgotten. Or maybe—no matter where you will make your new home—you might have a Torah scroll written in our memory. I am enclosing fifty American dollars, which I hope the messenger to whom I am giving this note will give to you.

I must hurry, because they have already ordered us to take off our clothes.

When I get to the Other World, I will convey your greetings to your holy ancestors and will ask them to intercede in your behalf so that your days may be long and happy.

Your servant,
Aryeh ben Leah Kornblit

P.S. My sister's children are now living with a Gentile family named Vasilevsky, near Gredig. Please take them away from there and turn them over to a Jewish family. Whatever happens, they must remain Jews. My wife, Sheva bat Chaya, was shot yesterday.

An old fifty-dollar bill fell out of the envelope.

The *rebbe* clasped the letter to his breast and carried it about with him wherever he went. When the war ended and he was brought to the United States, this letter went with him as his only possession. Thirty years have passed since then, and he has grown old, but he still cherishes it like a precious treasure.

Shortly after his arrival in the United States in the spring of 1946, the *rebbe* was invited to attend a *melaveh malkah* arranged by the Union of Hasidic Rabbis. The gathering was held in a hall on the Lower East Side of New York. Among the 500 rabbis and scions of rabbinic dynasties present there were many who, like the *rebbe* of Bluszow, had survived the Nazi death camps and had arrived in America only weeks or months before.

The audience sat in stunned silence as one Holocaust survivor after the other ascended the speaker's dais. As the frail figures, whose bodies and souls had passed through unspeakable tortures, urged the Jews of the United States not to despair but to have faith and understand that the hour of redemption could not be far distant, many in the audience could no longer restrain their tears. And when the *rebbe* of Bluszow, rose and, in a voice choked with sobs, read the letter from Aryeh ben Leah Kornblit, the hall resounded with bitter weeping.

After some calm had been restored, Rabbi Shapiro appealed to the audience to help him carry out the last wishes of his disciple. Few of those present at the *melaveh malkah* that night had amassed fortunes, but their response was generous, and eventually the scroll of the Law was completed and consecrated at the Yeshiva.

A few days before the ceremony, the writer of these lines called on Rabbi Shapiro at his home in Brooklyn. The rabbi, his hands trembling, held out the precious letter to him.

"Consider what strength God gives to His people," he exclaimed, as tears streamed down his cheeks. "Here you have a man who saw his wife shot, who himself was about to die and yet found it in his heart to think of those who would live after him — not only his sister's children, but also the people whom he would never know and who would hold his *Sefer Torah* in their arms.

"How great is our portion, how magnificent our heritage!"

Based on "Religiese Yidishe Velt," article by Nissan Gordon, in The Day-Jewish Journal, *May 14, 1953.*

Epilogue

by Gershon Jacobson

E very time I meet Simon Zuker I relive the nightmare of
the ghetto of Lodz. I hear the martyrs of Auschwitz
proclaim their last confession of faith and I see Jews —
men, women and children — march to their death beneath
the whips of SS men and *kapos*. Simon Zuker has an un-
usually picturesque manner of speech. When he describes
an event, or retells a saga of heroism and self-sacrifice,
you can see it all as if it had taken place only the day
before, and as if you yourself had been there.

"Thirty years and more have passed since the
destruction of European Jewry," Simon Zuker says, "and
we are still here. Why did we survive? Logically, we did
not have a chance — any more than did the Six Million
who are gone. Why, then, are we alive? The answer is
clear: we were meant to remain in order to serve as witnesses of the Holocaust, to preserve the memory of the loved
ones we have lost, and of a world that is no more.

"We will not, we dare not forget. For if we were ever
to forget, we ourselves would be guilty of murder. Hitler
killed the Six Million, but if we allow their memory to
fade, we, too, become their murderers. We must not permit our martyrs to die a second time. This is the reason
why we have founded the Zechor Institute."

Simon Zuker and Rabbi Leibel Cywiak founded the
Zechor Institute — "Zechor" means "Remember!" — in
order to help perpetuate the memory of European Jewry.

They have drawn up an ambitious program. The Institute is planning seminars and independent research in the history of the Holocaust, projects which will aid in the development of a systematized program of Holocaust studies at colleges, Jewish day schools and other educational institutions. The Institute also intends to launch a publication program: there will be textbooks on Holocaust history, and biographies of famous Jewish personages who were victims of the Nazi terror. The Institute will work to encourage Orthodox congregations and rabbinical organizations to plan memorial assemblies in keeping with the spirit of traditional Judaism.

Zuker is determined that the next generation of traditional Jews must not be permitted to grow up without any knowledge of the saintly grandfathers and grandmothers whom they were never able to meet in person.

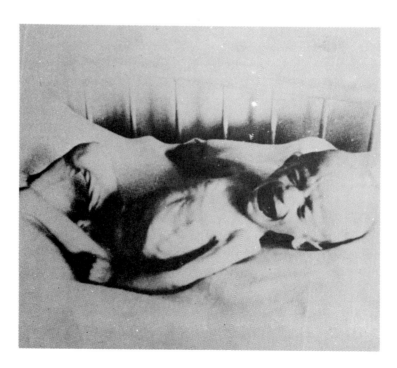

"We must not permit our martyrs to drown in a morass of indifference. And who else could preserve their sacred memory if not we, the last to be privileged to know the generation that is no more?"

"Non-religious Jews," Zuker continues, "have not forgotten the Six Million. Their memorial functions have had an impact even on our own religious schools. But the truly Orthodox Jew has not yet found a place, or a way, in which to express his sorrow in a manner meaningful to him. When an observant Orthodox Jew attends a memorial assembly arranged by Jews to whom religious tradition means little, if anything at all, he finds himself unable to enter fully into the spirit of the tribute these assemblies are intended to pay to the Six Million.

"The trouble is that, for some reason, the religious Jewish family is not yet psychologically ready to give the proper attention to the memory of these, the most recent

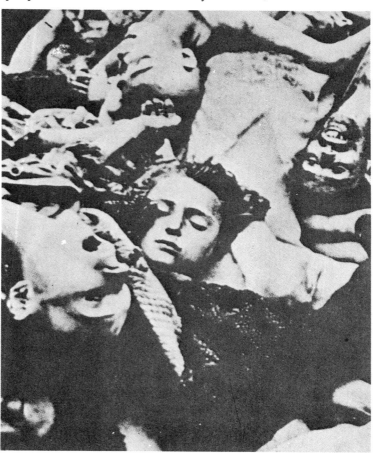

martyrs in our history. Oh, everybody observes Tisha B'Av. Even the youngest child knows what Tisha B'Av is all about. He sees his parents fast, sit on low stools and mourn, and he is told that it is for the Temple that was destroyed almost 2,000 years ago. But no day has yet been set aside for the express purpose of mourning the destruction of European Jewry in our own time."

Mr. Zuker remembers how 3,000 Jews from the ghetto of Lodz arrived in Auschwitz. At the head of the sad procession came Rabbi Abraham Silman. This was a son-in-law of R. Nehemiah Alter and thus a grandson by marriage of R. Judah Arye Leib Alter, author of the classic *Sefat Emet*. As the 8,000 filed through the gate of the camp, they were dealt blow upon blow with iron-tipped whips. This was just three weeks before Rosh HaShanah, 1944. The Jews asked Rabbi Silman how they should go about confessing their sins during the Days of Awe that year. "You don't have to confess anything," Rabbi Silman replied. "All you need to do is think of the One Above."

Simon Zuker's eyes are half closed. His voice sounds as if it was coming from another world. He speaks as if he were the advocate for the Six Million, pleading their case before the Heavenly Court of Justice.

"I ask you: how could I forget my own son Leibele, ten years old, how he came to me, prayer book in hand, for one last good-bye? Or my daughter, Hayye Sarah, who was only seven when they took her away? I saw men go to their death because they refused to part with their wives, and children murdered because they would not leave their parents or an aged grandmother. They clung to one another with a devotion beyond describing. Where in the lands of freedom today can one find such love between parents and their children? Are we supposed to put all this out of our minds?

"Most of the Jews in the ghetto of Lodz died of starvation because they refused to eat forbidden foods. No rabbi ever agreed to serve as a helper to the Nazi taskmasters. These were saintly people. Are we supposed to stop thinking about them?

"For thirty years we kept quiet before the Gentile world. We did not remind Christendom of its part in the murder of six million innocent human beings. The time has come for us to atone for thirty years of inactivity. As religious Jews, as living witnesses to a glorious, tragic past, we must teach, lecture and publish so that the world may know the whole story. If we will not do this, then the generations after us will neither know nor understand the heroism of the Holocaust generation. We have yet to tell, and to write, of the way Jews celebrated the Sabbath in the ghetto, how they died with the Word of God upon their lips. Are we to permit all this to be forgotten? The young people in our yeshivot are growing up with hardly any idea of how Jews in the camps and ghettoes hallowed the Name of God by their Jewish dignity, their saintly conduct until the very end.

"This is why we have created the institute to which we have given the name *Zechor* — Remember!

"To be sure," Mr. Zuker concluded, "it requires funds to carry on our program. But we will need something more than funds if we are to translate our plans into reality. We are in need of people who will give us not only of their substance, but also of their hearts, people who will work with all their might to see to it that the memory of our fallen will remain forever green in the hearts of future generations."

Based on article by Gershon Jacobson in Allgemeiner Journal, *Friday, May 21, 1976.*

קִינָה עַל חֻרְבָּן הָאַחֲרוֹן

Lamentation on the Holocaust

שמעון בה״ר י־הודה

He, who remembers those
   who were mindful of Him,
Each generation and its saintly martyrs —
   since the time Thou has chosen us —
May He remember the gruesome fate
   of the last generation.
                              Woe! What has happened to us!
All those who were swept away
   by the bloody flood —
All those who sacrificed their lives —
   all who drowned in the valley of tears,
May G-d think of them in the lands of Eternal Life.
   Forever may their memory be a blessing.

Lift your hands up to Him, woe O ye Heavens!
   woe over the best of Israel's tribes,
Communities and congregations, towns and districts,
   fraternities, foundations and all the houses of worship.

הַזּוֹכֵר מַזְכִּירָיו, דּוֹר דּוֹר וּקְדוֹשָׁיו,
מֵעֵת אֲשֶׁר אָז בְּחַרְתָּנוּ,
יִזְכּוֹר דֵּרָאוֹן, שֶׁל דּוֹר אַחֲרוֹן,
אוֹיָה מֶה הָיָה לָנוּ ...
שְׁטוּפֵי מַבּוּל־דָּם, שֶׁמָּכְרוּ נַפְשׁוֹתָם,
כָּל שְׁקוּעֵי עִמְקֵי־הַבָּכָא,
יִפְקְדֵם אֱ־לֹהִים, בְּאַרְצוֹת הַחַיִּים,
וַעֲדֵי עַד זִכְרָם לִבְרָכָה.

שְׂאוּ אֵלָיו כַּפַּיִם, אֲהָהּ, אִי שָׁמַיִם,
הוֹי עַל מֵיטַב שִׁבְטֵי־יִשְׂרָאֵל,
עֵדוֹת וּקְהִלּוֹת, עָרִים וּגְלִילוֹת,
חֲבוּרוֹת, מוֹסָדוֹת, כָּל מוֹעֲדֵי אֵ־ל,

I wished streams of water would pour out of my eyes
        towards the waterfalls of the rivers of tears—
For the millions of cremated corpses,
        consumed in the fires of destruction and horror.

For the princes of Torah, the pillars of Tradition,
        for the young flowers of priestly children,
For the diligent scholars, the teachers of men and women,
        and the precious youth attending schools,
The pious daughters, the old grandparents
        and their offspring, the little infants just born—
Everyone — thousand upon thousands,
        beloved in life, whom death did not part.

מִי יִתֵּן פַּלְגֵי מַיִם, תֵּרַדְנָה עֵינַיִם,
אֶל אַשְׁדוֹת נַחֲלֵי הַדְּמָעוֹת,
עֲלֵי אַלְפֵי אֲלָפִים גּוּפִים נִשְׂרָפִים,
בְּמוֹ־אֵשׁ הַחֻרְבָּן וּזְוָעוֹת.

וְעַל שָׂרֵי־הַתּוֹרָה, וּמַחֲזִיקֵי מָסוֹרָה,
וְעַל פִּרְחֵי הַכְּהֻנָּה הַצְּעִירִים,
וְעַל חוֹבְשֵׁי מִדְרָשׁוֹת, וּמוֹרִים וּמוֹרוֹת,
תִּינוֹקוֹת בֵּית־רַבָּן יַקִּירִים,
עַל בָּנוֹת בּוּטְחוֹת. וְסָבִים וְסָבוֹת,
וְעַל זַרְעָם וְטַפָּם שֶׁיָּלָדוּ,
וְגַם, לָרַבּוֹת, רְבָבוֹת נֶאֱהָבִים בַּחַיִּים,
בְּמוֹתָם לֹא נִפְרָדוּ.

Search for their blood!
    Take account of every driven leaf —
Of every life perished in the days of the holocaust —
    a total of six million dead.
Struck by lightning from the furious storm
    which devastated one full third
    of the cherished vineyards Thou didst so dearly love.
O Avenger of blood! Pray, do not erase
    the remembrance of their misery
    from the book which Thou hast written.

Remember every moan, every horrifying scream,
    when they were herded for slaughter —
All the rivers of blood, all the tear-stained faces:
    they must never be forgotten.

אֶת דָּמָם דְּרוֹשׁ, כִּי תִשָּׂא אֶת רֹאשׁ,
שֶׁל כָּל נִדָּף לְעָלִים הַטְּרוּפִים,
כָּל נַפְשׁוֹת־מֵת, בִּימֵי שֶׁבֶר וָשֵׁאת,
שִׁשָּׁה אַלְפֵי פְּעָמִים אֲלָפִים,
שְׁלִישִׁיָּה לְבָעֵר, בִּבְרַק זַעַם סוֹעֵר,
מִכַּרְמֵי הַחֶמֶד אָהַבְתָּ,
גּוֹאֵל הַדָּם, נָא זְכֹר צַעֲרָם,
אַל תִּמְחֶה מִסְפֵּר כָּתָבְתָּ.

זְכוֹר הַנְּאָקוֹת, וְרַעַשׁ צְעָקוֹת,
אָז יוּבְלוּ לָרֶצַח,
יְאוֹרֵי דְמֵיהֶם, וְדִמְעוֹת פְּנֵיהֶם,
לֹא תִשָּׁכַחְנָה לָנֶצַח,

Every horror, every sigh, every piercing cry
    from those torn asunder by hordes of dogs —
Remember them, count them,
    bind them into Thy bundle,
Till the day of Thy vengeance comes—
    to avenge their utter degradation.

In the barbarian's camp: pain, sickness,
    the anguish of mortified souls,
Insults and scoffing, shame and spit —
    searing wounds from merciless beatings —
Hunger, thirst, insanity, torture —
    stumbling of the faint whose strength was gone.
Every death-rattle of every single one,
    perishing in agony —
O, far be it from Thee,
    that this ever be forgotten:

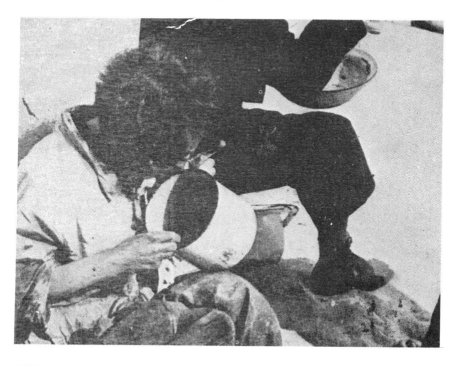

כָּל חִיל וּגְנִיחָה, וּנְהִי צְרִיחָה,
מִשְּׁדוּדֵי לַהֲקוֹת הַכְּלָבִים,
זְכוֹר וּסְפוֹר, בְּנֹאדְךָ צְרוֹר,
עַד עֵת נְקֹם עֶלְבּוֹן עֲלוּבִים.

בְּמַחֲנוֹת הַפְּרָאִים, כְּאֵב וּנְגָעִים,
וּפַחֵי נְפָשׁוֹת עֲגוּמוֹת,
חֶרְפּוֹת וּצְחוֹק, כְּלִימוֹת וָרֹק,
פִּצְעֵי הַכָּאוֹת אֵימוֹת,
וְרַעֲבוֹן, צִמָּאוֹן, שִׁגָּעוֹן, עִצָּבוֹן,
וְכִשְׁלוֹן נֶחֱשָׁלִים בְּלִי-כֹחַ,
וְכָל נַאֲקוֹת-חָלָל, מִכָּל יָחִיד אֻמְלָל,
חָלִילָה לְךָ מִלִּשְׁכֹּחַ.

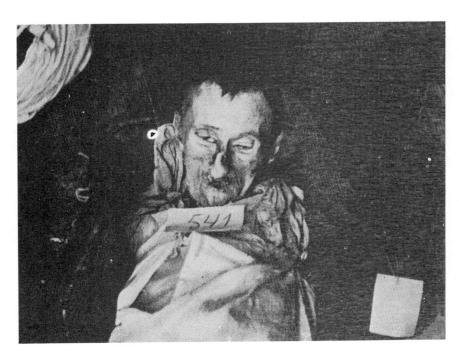

The smokestacks —
    heavy smokes from the furnaces,
Piles and piles of bones and limbs —
    halls of poison,
The roaring noise from the multitude,
    suffocating in the gas chambers —
The stench of the bodies — the emaciated corpses —
    fertilizers for the soil of the frivolous;
And how the tormentors turned
    human fat into soap
And their skin into decorations
    for their womenfolk.

(Remember) those savage leaders
    pointing their fingers —
To the right: slave labor! —
    to the left: the shadows of death!
(Remember) when the sharpshooter's shots
    felled the diggers, digging their own graves—
    to be buried still writing in agony.

וְתִימְרוֹת־עָשָׁן וְקִיטוֹר מִכִּבְשָׁן,
תְּלֵי־תִלִּים עֲצָמוֹת וְגִידִים,
וְחַדְרֵי הָרַעַל, קוֹל שְׁאָגוֹת
מִקְּהַל־הַנֶּחְנָקִים תּוֹךְ תָּאֵי הָאָדִים,
וְסִרְחוֹן גּוּפוֹת, וּגְוִיּוֹת סְגוּפוֹת,
גְּלַל־דִּמֶן אַדְמַת נוֹאֲצִים,
אֵיךְ הָפְכוּ טוֹרְפֵיהֶם, לִבְרִית חֶלְבֵּיהֶם,
וְעוֹר־אִישׁ לְקִשּׁוּטֵי הַנָּשִׁים.

וּקְרִיצַת אֶצְבָּעוֹת, שֶׁל רָאשֵׁי־הַפְּרָעוֹת,
לִימִין שֶׁעְבוּד־פֶּרַךְ, צַלָמוֹת לִשְׂמֹאל,
וְאֵיךְ יָרוּ יְרִיּוֹת עַל חוֹפְרֵי הַבּוֹרוֹת,
בְּיִסּוּרֵי חִבּוּט־קֶבֶר הוֹרְדוּם שְׁאוֹל,

And — how they raped our sisters —
  mutilated our daughters —
And poisoned medicine
  from cruel doctors.
And the fugitives! In holes and hide-outs —
  and their children abandoned in idolatrous homes.

Sheep without blemish —
  the blood of our captive children,
Offered upon the mighty altar;
  woe! It was Thy loving servant's lifeless flesh;
Who could count the saintly flock?
  May their fire never go out,
For they stood Thy test—
  they were Sanctifiers of Thy Name.
They, who with the cry of "Sh'ma Yisroel!"
  gave up their lives for God,
  so that He may gather them in.
Until the very last believing in His justice,
  singing aloud the song of faith "Anee Maamin"

אֵיךְ עֻנּוּ אֲחִיּוֹתֵינוּ, וְסֹרְסוּ בְּנוֹתֵינוּ,
כּוֹסוֹת־תַּרְעֵלָה מִידֵי רוֹפְאִים אַכְזָרִים,
וּפְלִיטֵי הַשְּׂרִידִים בִּמְחִלּוֹת וּסְתָרִים,
וְטִמְיוֹן יְלָדִים בְּבָתֵּי שְׁמַד־כְּמָרִים.

שֶׁה־תָמִים לָעוֹלָה, דַּם בְּנֵי הַגּוֹלָה,
הוֹי אֲרִיאֵל מִנִּבְלַת חֲסִידֶיךָ
צֹאן־קְדָשִׁים מִי יִמְנֶה, אֲשֶׁר אִשָּׁם לֹא תִכְבֶּה,
בְּחוּנֶיךָ הָיוּ מְקַדְּשֵׁי שְׁמֶךָ,
בְּקוֹל שְׁמַע יִשְׂרָאֵל מָסְרוּ נֶפֶשׁ לָאֵ־ל,
שֶׁהוּא יַאַסְפֵם, וְעַד יוֹם אַחֲרוֹן
הִצְדִּיקוּ דִין, וְאַף אֲנִי מַאֲמִין עָנוּ,
וְשָׁרוּ שִׁירַת בִּטָּחוֹן.

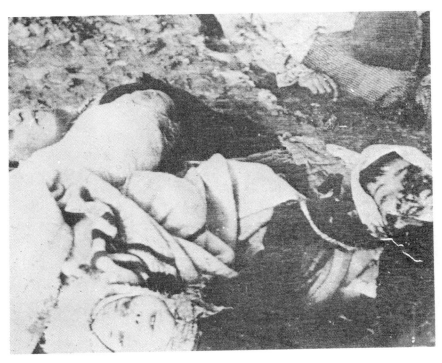

What is left now: a people, bewildered like orphans —
    no graves to pray at —
No tombstones to weep at
    the tears of our sacred hearts.
Their sacrificial blood is their memorial —
    the blood which will forever be boiling,
Which will never be forgotten;
    and the mountains of ashes from their "Akeidah,"
Yea, all the ash-piles at the altars
    shall be their lasting tribute.

Who could express Yisroel's torment,
    its mind disturbed by misery —
What's left of its shine reduced to tiny bits —
    its greatness sorely crushed today
O living God! o' Merciful One!
    Comfort Thy congregation
    which yearns so much for Thee.
Cause a new light to shine forth,
    let rays of glory glow.
And may God's sacred spirit
    once more rest upon us.

וּבְכֵן נִשְׁאַר עַם, כְּיַתּוֹם נִדְהָם,
בְּלִי קְבָרִים לְהִשְׁתַּטֵּחַ,
וְלֹא מַצֵּבוֹת, אֵיפֹה לִבְכּוֹת,
יָבֹשׁוּ לֵבָב רוֹתֵחַ,
רַק נִסְכֵּי־הַדָּם, אַזְכָּרוֹתָם,
תּוֹסְסִים בְּלִי שׁוֹכֵחַ,
וְהָרֵי אֶפְרֵי עֲקֵדָתָם,
תְּרוּמוֹת דִּשְׁנֵי מִזְבֵּחַ.

מִי יְמַלֵּל, צַעַר יִשְׂרָאֵל,
אֲשֶׁר דַּעְתּוֹ מִכְּאֵב נִטְרֶפֶת,
וּשְׁאֵרִית הַפְּאֵר, כִּמְעַט מִזְעֵיר,
וְאֵיךְ קוֹמָתָה הַיּוֹם נִכְפֶּפֶת,
אֵ־ל חַי מְרַחֵם, עֲדָתְךָ נַחֵם,
אֲשֶׁר לְךָ מְאֹד נִכְסֶפֶת,
אוֹר־חָדָשׁ תַּזְרִיחַ, קַרְנֵי־הוֹד תַּצְמִיחַ,
וְרוּחַ אֱ־לֹהִים מְרַחֶפֶת.

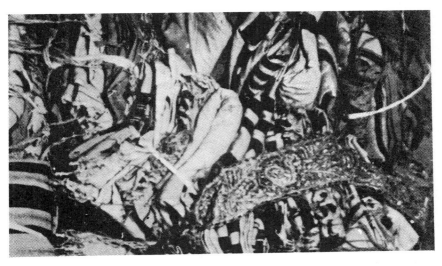

Footnotes

1. Rabbi Baruch Yarhar, *Bet Komarno*, p. 174.

2. Yehoash Alfrovi, *Sefer Wieliczka*, p. 137.

3. Moshe Grynstein, *Sefer Piotrkov*, p. 137.

4. Sefer Lukow, p. 491.

5. Mottel Deinbart, *Sefer Frampol*, p. 231.

6. Eliezer Langer, *Sefer Apta*, p. 231.)

7. This hymn (the words comprise the twelfth of the Thirteen Articles of Faith, which are part of the daily Morning Service) had its origins in the Warsaw ghetto. The music was composed by the singer-composer Azriel David Fastag, an adherent of the rabbinic dynasty of Modzitz. Modzitzer Hasidim have composed *niggunim* (melodies) that are sung by Hasidim the world over. The first *rebbe* of the dynasty, R. Israel (d. 1921), was known as the composer of many Hasidic melodies.

8. Stubendienst, Room order service.

9. Talmudist and Hasidic rabbi (1765-1827), who was also active as a merchant and pharmacist.

10. Eliezer Unger, *Zakhor*, p. 24.

11. Chaim Lieberman, *Heilike Massim* in *Jewish Daily Forward*, May 5, 1947.

12. Hillel Zeitlin (1872-1942) was reared in a Hasidic environment but early came under the influence of modern Hebrew writers. He became an editor of the Hebrew journal *HaZ'man* but later wrote mostly in Yiddish. A student of Jewish mysticism and Hasidism, he was known for his devoutness in his later years. He died in Treblinka.

13. Moshe Malz, *Sefer Sokol*, p. 293.

14. B. Goldberg, *Sefer Linovice*, p. 99.

15. *Leviticus* 18:5.

16. Babylonian Talmud, *Yoma* 85b, *Sanhedrin* 74a.

17. Menashe Unger, *Sefer Kedoshim*, p. 344-45.

18. Moshe Prager, *Eleh she-lo Nichneu*, Vol. I, p. 177.

19. Based on an account by Rabbi Kalman Farber in *Sefer Vieliko*.

20. Israel Gutman, Auaskim *Ve-Efer* Afanan *Auschwitz*, p.86.

21. Yechiel Granetstein, *Sefer Pitrkon*, p. 859.

22. Menashe Unger, *Sefer Kadoshim*, pp. 344-45.

23. Jacob Kushitzky, *Pinkas Kletzk*, p. 156.

24. Menashe Unger, *Der geistige Vidershtand*, p. 184.

25. Hillel Seidman, *Eleh Ezkarah*, Vol. I, p. 246.

26. Jacob Rasson, *Mir Velen Leven*.

27. Moshe Prager, *Eleh She-Lo Nichna'h*, Vol. II, p.175.

28. In *Togbuch fun Vilner Ghetto*, New York, YIVO, 1961, p. 241.

29. Eliezer Yerushalmi, *Pinkas Siauliai*, p. 300.

30. Leib Garfinkel, *Kovna: HaYehudit L'Harvono*.

31. Wolf Yasni, *Geshikhte fun Yiden in Lodz*, Vol. II, p. 254.

32. Reuven Sharid, *Sefer Dembitz*, pp. 144-45.

33. Hillel Seidman, *Eleh Ezkerah*, Vol. III, p. 126.